*T*o our beautiful son Asher. You inspire us to be better people and the best parents we can possibly be. All of the words in this book fall short of expressing how much we love you.

# www.mascotbooks.com

*Our Happy Divorce*

Cover design by Cynthia Creative & Co

**For more information, please contact:**
Mascot Books
620 Herndon Parkway #320
Herndon, VA 20170
info@mascotbooks.com

**CPSIA Code:** PRFRE0819A
**Library of Congress Control Number:** 2019905258
**ISBN-13:** 978-1-63177-997-8

Printed in Canada

# Our Happy Divorce

## HOW ENDING OUR MARRIAGE BROUGHT US TOGETHER

## NIKKI DEBARTOLO *and* BENJAMIN HELDFOND

# INTRODUCTION

*W*e are ordinary people who have accomplished something extraordinary.

When our marriage ended, we were frightened of what the future looked like for our family. We didn't want to get stuck where we were, unable to move past the worst moments in our relationship. We worried that no matter how carefully we tried to avoid it, we'd end up using our son, Asher, as a pawn or a bargaining chip. When we looked for models of divorce and post-divorce parenting that fit our needs, we realized that we were really on our own.

Anyone with betting odds would have closed the book on us, but we knew our marriage was just a chapter in our story together. When the marriage chapter was over, we decided that there were going to be more chapters ahead of us, even if we had to write them ourselves. Our happy divorce began when we realized that, contrary to popular wisdom, we could have the thing we wanted most: What is best for Asher. We were sure that we could make it work—we just had to sacrifice every last shred of pride, ego, fear, control, and selfishness in ourselves. We had to focus everything, from the biggest decisions to the smallest details, through that lens.

We fashioned new tools when we realized the ones that existed weren't working. We sidestepped a lot of the booby traps that make most divorces acrimonious. We did a lot of work on ourselves, our relationship, and our understanding of the world. We've gotten incredible results, witnessed amazing personal growth in ourselves and each other, and strengthened our bonds together and with our extended families. Most importantly, Asher has flourished.

What we have built over the past years is a huge testament to how much we love our son, how hard we were willing to work when everything looked the worst, and how much support we were able to draw from each other and our incredible families.

We're not lawyers, psychiatrists, or divorce counselors. This is just what we did, and what happened as a result. We decided to tell our story for many reasons, but the most important one is that we'd love to help others. When we started our divorce process, we would have given anything for just a single example of the best case, a single shred of hope that it could possibly work out well.

No one would have come to us for relationship advice when we were married, but many have after our divorce. We get calls from family, friends, and acquaintances facing their own divorces or relationships problems, asking us how we made it all work so beautifully. As our modern family has blossomed and withstood tests and time, even some of our more open initial detractors have started shyly asking us how we did it. People want help. Despite the odds, we orchestrated a divorce that made us and everyone we love happier and healthier. While some people still don't understand our modern family structure, they are fascinated by our results. What we have isn't the new normal yet, but people are longing for it, and we'd love to see it become the divorce default.

We could have titled this book *The Good Divorce*, but we chose *Our Happy Divorce* for a reason. We want to make it clear that we've learned that it's possible not only to survive a divorce, but to emerge from it better in every way. We're genuinely happier. It took good intentions, loving support, and patience. There were setbacks and steps forward. Now, though, our lives are better than ever—ours, our new families', and our son's. It truly is the easier, softer way. It has been a journey that has taught us to find a different kind of love for each other. Trust us. If we could do it, you can do it.

*Nikki DeBartolo*
*& Ben Heldfond*

# Ben

Living in a hotel isn't so bad. Actually, it was pretty cool at first, before I'd tried everything on the room service menu and watched everything on pay-per-view. Leaving my room for the first leg of my new daily commute that morning, though, I had to admit that the novelty had worn off over the past few months. Now, the most exciting days were when the hotel added a new movie into the rental rotation.

The clock on my dash lit up as I started the car—six-thirty on the dot. Our home was less than five miles from my room at the Renaissance, no more than fifteen minutes in the worst traffic, but I didn't play fast and loose with the timing. Asher's sleep schedule was downright robotic. He went to bed every evening exactly at eight and woke up, without fail, between 6:55 and 7:10. I always gave myself at least an extra ten-minute buffer to get inside and get settled.

I didn't always make it over for bedtime, but Nikki would cover for me on those nights, letting Asher know I was at a meeting or a business dinner. I was always there when he woke up in the morning, though. I snuck into the house to preserve the illusion that I was still living there. My son was only three, still young enough that Nikki and I could try to hide the growing rift between us.

Getting out of the car was like jumping into a sauna. My shirt was already sticking to my back, and the sun hadn't even fully risen yet.

"Tampa," I cursed under my breath.

I was in a weird mood already. The entire time I'd been out of the house, Nikki and I had been talking about getting back together and giving it (yet another) shot. I had almost been completely convinced, before last night. In the space of one breath, Nikki had gone from telling me how much she loved me and how much she wanted to work on the relationship to informing me she would be in L.A. that weekend. In the back of my mind, all I could think was that these were just words that I had heard before and nothing was going to change. Our relationship had gone insane—not violent or nasty, but insane like watching your favorite movie for the hundredth time and thinking the ending was going to be different this time.

So, that morning, I was already a little on edge and confused as I walked into the house. Luckily, Asher and I are creatures of habit, and our morning routine did not let me down: a big smile, a big hug, and Shrek Eggo waffles before work and school.

"Hey buddy!" I boomed as he came into the kitchen.

"Dad!" Asher grinned.

I popped the Eggos into the toaster and grabbed the newspaper, leaning up against the counter. My phone buzzed steadily beside me, and I multitasked happily between work emails, my son, and sport scores.

Too soon, Asher finished his breakfast and ran to get his backpack. I wrapped him up in a bear hug and watched as he and the babysitter left for school.

The happy, homey feel dissipated behind them. I was alone in the house, feeling out of sorts again. I wandered aimlessly around the kitchen, trying to remember what specific event had spurred me to move out. To this day, I honestly don't remember.

Nikki and I never really fought. Over time, our marriage had just devolved; it felt like living with a roommate. It was awkward, and it wasn't fun anymore. Instead of being adults and honestly asking ourselves what we were doing, we'd just swept things under the rug while hoping our relationship would miraculously mend. We'd both suspected our differences were too big to solve, so we'd stopped communicating at all.

We were in limbo now. On some level, we both knew that we needed to do something different, but we were too proud and stubborn to admit defeat. We were scared to even face the idea. We didn't want to subject our son to a divorce. We wanted to provide Asher with a two-parent household; we wanted to stay together for him. We considered divorce a failure, and we didn't want to fail ourselves, our families, our child.

I decided to grab some fresh clothes and some paperwork to take back to the hotel with me, so I walked into my office—well, the office that I'd once occupied. Since I'd been gone, Nikki had quickly made it her own. I sat down at the desk in front of my computer, but I was distracted. The two brain cells I had left in my head began throwing stones at each other.

You owe it to the marriage and your son to not throw in the towel.

Are you crazy? What is going to be different?

Absentmindedly, I started riffling through a stack of papers on the desk. I stopped short at the sight of one of Nikki's world-famous handwritten calendars.

Nikki has always been an organizational powerhouse, and these calendars were fine-tuned, well-choreographed masterpieces. This coming weekend, of course, showed her trip to L.A. to work on her jewelry business—an irritating reminder. As my eyes trailed further down the calendar, though, I could feel the blood rushing to my head and my heart pounding through my chest. Irritation turned to fury.

She was scheduled to be gone for the next four weekends.

How the fuck are we going to work on our relationship if she's living a totally separate life in L.A.?

The thought struck me like divine intervention. Nikki had done a great job telling me exactly what I wanted to hear, but none of it lined up with her actions. She wasn't here doing the work to mend this, and she clearly wasn't planning to schedule it in. My house wasn't mine, my marriage wasn't mine—even my life didn't feel like my own.

Ten years of trying to fit a square peg into a round hole had taken its toll. I was depressed and hurt. My ego was shattered. I was done. I didn't call or leave a letter. I left my wedding ring on top of the stack of mail and walked away, bitter and out for blood.

# Nikki

I dropped my gym bag by the front door, exhausted and exhilarated by my morning. I was excited to get cleaned up, do some work, and see Asher.

I walked into the kitchen and grabbed a drink out of the fridge, meandering towards the pile of mail stacked underneath my calendar. The pile beckoned, literally glittering in the late afternoon sunlight that bounced off the bay and in through the kitchen window.

The mail was…gold?

My stomach dropped to my feet as my brain connected the abandoned wedding band to Ben's message. My marriage was over.

Ben and I had fought before; he had even moved out of our home before. We'd been seeing professionals, trying to make it work. It was frustrating and fruitless, but I'd never truly considered what it would feel like if it didn't work. The idea that we were actually speeding towards a divorce hadn't been real for me until that nauseating moment.

My very first thought was, *Oh shit—I need to fix this*. My gut instinct was to blame myself entirely. I'd ruined everything, and it was my job to make it right and make the marriage work.

Crying, I called Lisa, my eldest sister. Lisa had gotten back from her honeymoon with her new husband, Don, just the day before, but she came over to my house and was on the phone with Ben right away. Over the years, Ben had grown as close to my family as anyone could possibly get. He trusted their judgment and listened to their advice, and they'd been able to talk us both through issues in our marriage before. Lisa hung up with tears in her own eyes; he wasn't budging.

Sitting on the floor next to Lisa, I wondered what memories Asher would have as an adult of watching Ben and me interact. I wondered how I could teach him how to fight for what was important to him if Ben and I couldn't show him through our marriage. I kept repeating that I wanted us to be a family, that I wanted Ben back. Finally, Lisa looked over and gently told me she didn't think that was what I really wanted at all.

I was stunned—that was one of the most ridiculous things I'd ever heard. Of course, that's what I wanted! It wouldn't make any sense for me to want anything different—right?

Still reeling and wondering how I could win Ben back, I packed Asher up and established camp at Lisa and Don's home. I'm sure Don hadn't expected their household to grow so suddenly, but he welcomed us. He earned his spot in the family and everyone's hearts pretty quickly, joking about getting a second wife out of the deal and treating Asher like his own. Lisa and Don let Asher choose his own playroom in their new house, and he picked the biggest one; Don ordered a giant rug printed like a football field for Asher. I was grateful to my entire family for the space to think, cry, and do whatever I needed to do to process everything. Playing full family football games on the cushy rug with Asher every night after dinner, I started to breathe easier. Ben and I weren't the only ones who loved Asher more than anything in the world. No matter what, making sure Asher felt safe and supported and happy was at the top of everyone's list.

It took me several weeks to start coming to terms with the fact that I had tried to stay married for all the wrong reasons. As scared as I was, particularly for Asher, my sister had been right: I did want the divorce. I admitted to myself that if I had really wanted to stay in the marriage, I would have been acting differently—and Ben would have too. My mother used to say, "If you don't love their guts, it's never going to work." Ben and I hadn't acted like two people who loved each other's guts in a very long time.

I finally began to understand what was happening. After seven years of a marriage that never quite fit right, Ben and I were done—angry, bitter, incapable of communicating, done. We couldn't stay married, and we refused to hurt our son. It seemed like an impossible problem to solve. The legal battle alone was going to be public and embarrassing. Our families would hate each other, and we'd really hate each other. Staying together for Asher, locked in some miserable death grip, wasn't possible—we'd already tried. Even if it was, we knew it would still hurt him; there was no way we could give him the life that he deserved with how toxic we were becoming towards each other.

When Ben and I met, I was twenty-one years old. I loved to have fun with my friends, and I was working hard at my job. I was still just starting to explore what being an adult meant, like most twenty-one-year olds. Two months after I started dating Ben, my family went through a major upheaval, and my world changed rapidly. I was just getting to know Ben when the relationship shifted. Almost overnight, I went from smitten with puppy-love to seeing him as a source of stability in a very chaotic period. We had so much fun together and I loved him, but we'd never had the easiest of relationships. Everything else in life had been so complicated, and I never had the chance to catch my breath and look at the bigger picture. When we got married two years after we met, I had been coasting through all the way to the altar in many ways.

After I'd spent a lot of time thinking, I could see that Ben and I had gotten married when we were very young and that we'd matured in different ways, separate from one another. Like Lisa and Don, we were both very strong people—but unlike them, our individual strengths didn't complement each other's. We didn't make one another stronger, at least not as a couple.

It was difficult to admit to myself. Having this marriage crumble was one of my first major experiences with not being able to fix something in my personal life. I realized that I'd never really figured out what type of constant compromise and effort it would take to make a marriage work. I'd also never found the boundaries of my relationships. I'd been testing the limits, and I'd thought I'd be able to fix anything I broke along the way. I learned the emotional difference between strained and shattered, and it became a period of quick and painful personal growth.

Ben and I are similar in many ways, but we usually react to stressful situations very differently. In crisis mode, I tend to be demonstrative, while Ben's MO is to get almost preternaturally calm. Leaving his ring on the counter was an uncharacteristically dramatic gesture for him, but I wasn't about to change my methods. It would be almost impossible to hide things or keep secrets from my family even if I wanted to. We are the biggest advocates and best sounding boards for each other; we talk about everything, and we work together to solve issues. When one of us has a problem, we all have a problem.

It wasn't that Ben and I had pretended to be the perfect couple. Anyone close to us had concerns about our relationship, just like we did. My family had never said anything to me, but I knew they had all noticed that Ben and I rarely seemed to be together as a couple anymore. Once Asher was born, it seemed like everything was getting better, and in some ways it was. We both admired each other in our roles as parents—Ben was an amazing dad from the first moments, and he helped me through my fear into becoming the mom I always wanted to be. We were both great parents, but as Asher grew older, the perfect fit of these new roles just highlighted how itchy and uncomfortable our husband and wife suits had become. I loved having Asher with me, and he became my sole focus. Ben was playing the man of the house role; he went to work, came home, and then did his own thing. We didn't interact anymore; we were just ships in the night.

Some part of me had thought that my relationship with Ben was safe because we'd never really fought. My family is full of very emotional people, and we can't hide any sentiment, happy or sad. In our house growing up, we would yell and scream if we were mad at someone and get everything off our chests and then it was over. Five minutes later, we'd be discussing what we wanted for dinner. Fighting never felt like a big deal; it seemed normal to me. In my heart, I knew that my family's volatility was fueled by a real desire to communicate. My parents always talked things through when they faced difficult situations. Some things were quiet, some things were not, but the point was that they were facing it together. Growing up, my sisters and I didn't take part in every single discussion in their marriage, but we heard our fair share. We all knew that no matter what was wrong, they'd work to solve it.

In comparison with my family, though, Ben had never heard his parents fight before they decided to get a divorce. They always acted like everything was fine—until it wasn't. I guess our marriage had followed that same path.

My father believes that God creates the right marriage for each of us in heaven before we're even born, and that when He throws our soulmate in front of us, we can't turn it down. Both of my older sisters had been very vocal about never wanting to get married since we were young. We were all shocked when they changed their minds, but they'd stumbled on the husbands meant for them along their paths.

Growing up, my middle sister Tiffanie was wrapped up in books and poems and a really romantic idea of the life she wanted. A husband was absolutely not in the plan—until her first day of acting class, when a certain guy walked in. She was done. She actually heard a voice inside her head, like in the movies, clearly telling her she was going to marry him. She fell madly in love with Scott right then and there. However, there was a girlfriend and graduate school standing in their way, so Tiffanie wrote a screenplay about her relationship with Scott. It was actually picked up and made into a movie, and they met back up and watched the premier together. That was that; they've been together ever since. They're creative and adventurous together, and it's grown and shifted with them over decades. Tiffanie realized, the moment she saw Scott, her romantic ideas about life had space for one more, as long as it was him.

Lisa held strong to her anti-marriage stance into her late thirties, pretty much minutes before my own marriage unraveled. She'd just gotten out of a long-term relationship with a man she never considered changing her views for—and then Don swept into her life like a storm. He spotted her across a crowded room and they met for ten seconds—but it must have been a pretty significant ten seconds. He went home, finished filing for divorce, and three months later, Lisa and Don were married.

My family had gotten all worked up when they announced their marriage news; it was very dramatic, and no one knew what to think. We didn't know Don. Was this a prank? Were supposed to be scandalized? There were lots of questions. Don jokes now that he owes me big time, since he was only saved from the full (and possibly eternal) DeBartolo wrath by Ben and me. When my family found out about my upcoming divorce, they switched targets, and Don and Lisa were left to love each other in peace.

Watching the newlyweds interact, I started thinking differently about marriage and what it meant to compliment your spouse in ways I'd never considered before. Lisa had always been so strong and independent, and she was positive she would hate being married. As children, we only really saw very traditional Italian Catholic marriages, where the men were in charge and the women did what was expected of them. Don, however, was the exact opposite of the men we had known growing up. He was older, self-assured, and only wanted to make Lisa happy. Like Ben, Lisa's ex-boyfriend had worked for my father, which made him belong more to the family at large than to just Lisa. Don was a musician, and he didn't have any interest in proving himself in the business arena. He already knew who he was, and Lisa knew who she was—they had fallen head-over-heels for the people they were, not the people they could potentially become. They weren't identical or even that similar in any way, and it didn't matter: They were just wholly compatible as a couple. They had things they could teach each other. Their strengths didn't compete, and they didn't share the same weak spots. They were both strong people apart, and they were even stronger together.

I started to realize that Ben and I both had our share of responsibility to take for the ending of our marriage. It really had taken two to break it. Ben and I had very different needs, and neither of us had been taken care of. Ben could be as needy as a child. I had enjoyed nurturing him that way when we first met, but I had a real baby now. When I get sick or feel bad, I keep moving and fight my way back to better; Ben can lie around and mope, and I'd started to resent him for it. I had gotten tired of taking care of him when he didn't seem to want to take care of himself, and I'd started to resent a lack of reciprocity. Ben wasn't always interested in the people around him, and I had felt ignored more often than I'd cared to admit.

As much as we'd denied it to ourselves and each other, Ben and I had feared this moment and tried to fight it for a long time. We did a lot over the years to try to make it work, but in the end, it was time to let it go. By the time Ben and I met again to discuss how we would move forward, I had come to terms with a lot.

I knew I needed to forgive myself to start moving forward, which was easier said than done. I knew we had been good friends in the beginning, and any pre-marriage professional probably would have counseled us to stay that way. I'm so happy we never asked, because I would have gone through the worst divorce in the world if it meant still having Asher.

# Ben

I t would be nice if I could tell you that Nikki and I calmly and lovingly turned to each other one day, hugged, and parted ways wordlessly. There are some people who just seem to have evolved to a higher spiritual plane, who can immediately empathize with the inner conflicts of someone who cuts them off in traffic. Except that's not our story, and that's not us. We live in the real world. We have flaws. We get frustrated and angry and exhausted. We have every emotion, and we're actually both incredibly stubborn and single-minded (which, spoiler, turned out to be keys to our divorce success). We're both very strong, type-A personalities, and we can both be self-indulgent at times. We both do what we like to do, when we like to do it, and the end of our marriage was like a checklist of how rarely those visions matched.

Before we started our happy divorce, I was in an ugly place and I was anxious to make it uglier. I had to hit rock bottom and realize exactly how bad things could get if we didn't find a radical new path. I had to forgive Nikki, which meant I had to take accountability for the role I had played in the breakdown and come to terms with the fact that my actions and behavior revealed a man who had stopped working on himself. Before we could even sit down together and decide that our son's happiness was so important to us both that we could work through anything else, I had to take time to reflect.

Our breakup had every ingredient lined up to make a life-ruining dish. It could easily have been as messy and awful and sad as any in history—our last days certainly were. Years of bad communication and ignoring issues had taken their toll on us. It wasn't fun anymore, and we were both limping through, isolated from each other and hurt all the time. There were a hundred thousand little cuts on both sides, mostly unintentional, but a few that weren't. There was also that last straw, the single moment when my ego was shattered and I was done.

I think that done moment is when most people surrender to the divorce machine. I did; I walked out the door that day and started searching for the cruelest divorce attorney available, an absolute shark. Done is pointing the finger at the other person and saying it is all their fault. Done is angry and bitter and out for blood—and I was all those things and more. I was positive this was all Nikki's fault, and she was going to pay for fucking up my life. Done is the foundation that the lawyers and the courts and the professionals build divorces on, providing results that only the lawyers benefit from. Before Nikki and I even imagined embarking on our experiment in alternative divorce, I had started building a very standard divorce for us from done. I was furious and ready to make this a huge, public disaster. We were on the perfect track to blow it all up.

I put the most heartless, ruthless lawyer I could find on retainer. I told him I wanted to take the prenup and shove it in her face, and he told me it looked like there was a hole in it big enough to drive an eighteen-wheeler through. Soon enough, he'd sent me a twenty-five-page report all about the prenup.

I sat on it for three weeks. Understand, I am the multitasking king. I work best when I'm juggling eight things, rubbing my tummy, and tapping my head—there's never "not enough time" to get something done when I'm amped up on it. I was fueled by anger and I wanted to hurt Nikki, and I knew that divorce lawyer's report was my weapon.

But I kept finding reasons not to crack it open.

Finally, on a plane from L.A. back to Tampa, I ran out of excuses and decided it was time to read it. I got through three pages, shut it, and never opened it again.

The report was disgusting; it had only taken those three pages to make me physically nauseous. It wasn't a hatchet job—it was a full chainsaw massacre. Suddenly, I knew why I'd been avoiding it. Deep down, I'd been rightfully terrified—not even necessarily by what I knew it would say, but by what reading it would mean. Those three pages gave me a very clear vision of how ugly the future could be—my future, Nikki's future, the future of the divorce, and most importantly, Asher's future. I'd been making plans with huge emotional costs attached. I knew Asher was going to be the one stuck paying most of that hefty bill for something that wasn't his decision, something he had no say in. Continuing down this path for just one more page, much less an entire acrimonious divorce, would be the biggest mistake of my life.

It was a hard slap in the face to realize for the first time how easily this could turn out just like my parents' bitter divorce—maybe even worse. Their marriage had ended suddenly, but the pain and anger lasted for years and left scars on us all. My parents never shared with my siblings and me their reasons and impetus for ending their marriage. I still don't know why it happened. I know they made a conscious decision to spare us those details, but we were exposed to so much of the ugliness of the fallout. I felt like each parent fed us poison, hoping the other would die. I didn't want to poison Asher the same way.

Parents inadvertently end up using their children as blocking and tackling tools frequently in failed and failing marriages. I know it was incredibly difficult for me to process my own feelings and resentment in the beginning. If I had built a divorce and started a new life from that done moment, it could easily have blinded me to how I was passing on this emotional damage to my child. Approaching Nikki with bitterness and hatred, it would have even seemed like I was doing Asher a favor, exposing his mother for the person I would have convinced myself she was. One of my duties as a parent is to teach my child how to protect himself from people who will hurt him. If I had let myself get caught in that done moment for years, poisoning my son with my disappointment in his mother wouldn't have felt like an excuse for validating my own pain. It would have felt like wisely advising him against making the same mistake of choosing to love and trust a person who could hurt him too.

And how could I have expected Nikki not to poison Asher towards me, trying to protect him the same way? I was gearing up to try to punish and destroy her, the mother of my child, someone I'd committed to taking care of and loving forever. Successful or not, it would have changed who I was, inherently, as a person. How could I reasonably expect her to trust me not to turn on Asher at some point? If I chose to execute on this bitterness, knowingly subjecting my son to the consequences, could I even reasonably trust myself?

Witnessing how hurt and unhappy my parents' divorce made my mother was one of the worst experiences of the whole thing for me. At her core, my mother stayed true to who she was and always will be—an intensely caring, loving woman, the most unselfish person I have ever met. After the divorce, she completed her MBA at Berkeley and constantly worked on improving herself and expanding her skills—all while raising four young kids alone and never missing a single one of our events. There were other changes, though, and her relationship with my dad after he moved out was a visible strain on her happiness for a very long time.

My siblings and I were exposed to many negative details that were difficult for us to process. Separating finances and assets during a divorce are common minefields, ones I had been directly targeting in my plan to hurt Nikki. Remembering the pain on my mother's face when she told us my father had taken a banquet table, an heirloom that had been in her family for generations, opened my eyes to what I'd be exposing Asher to. I'd felt so uncomfortable and awkward about witnessing those hurtful moments as a child. I really hadn't wanted to think of either of my parents as bad people, and I was positive I did not want my son to have to face the same awful feelings.

My father moved out when I was thirteen, two weeks before my bar mitzvah, and my parents weren't able to establish even a functional relationship with each other afterwards, which I quickly starting using to my advantage. I was a born manipulator, and I had realized as a very young kid how useful it was that adults found me charming and adorable. Where they saw charisma, I saw a way to use my big personality to get whatever I wanted. I had always gotten away with murder, and now my siblings and I suddenly had all sorts of blind spots to hide in. My parents were in a new situation with no guidance, and they both felt insecure that my siblings and I would prefer the other parent, which I exploited by playing them off each other. They had effectively stopped communicating, so they couldn't check to verify my whereabouts or if I was being truthful about house rules or curfews. I snuck around and exploited all of it for my own ends.

Even when I'd get in trouble, my parents would rush to take care of it, and I never faced any serious consequences—I don't think I ever even processed that consequences were real. I barely graduated high school. I went to a very good private school and got pretty good grades, but I lied and cheated my way through. I was caught faking the required community service hours, and the administration was ready to kick me out. The doors to college would have been closed, and Berkeley would have rescinded my acceptance. I walked across the stage at graduation and opened an empty diploma folder, but I still don't remember being all that concerned. I have no idea to this day how my mother resolved it—that's how separated I was from a sense of consequence. She handled it. They fixed it like I knew they would, like they always did, and I learned nothing except that it's easier to not get caught.

I had already started drinking and smoking pot before my parents got divorced, and now I had way more space to get into whatever I wanted. My brother and I lived in the basements of both parents' homes, which had been converted into two-room suites with separate entrances. I was partying every night. When I got to college, everything was wide open. This complete freedom and my own wildness brought me to the point where I didn't think anything bad would happen to me if I tried heroin. No, really. I knew exactly what it was, how powerful it was, but I was absolutely unable to process that those consequences—any consequences—could ever apply to me.

The first time I tried heroin, I knew it was the answer to all my problems. It was the feeling that I had always been looking for—because I felt nothing. I didn't feel pain or inadequacy. I felt completely numb, and everything was quiet.

I spent the next two years trying to capture that same feeling again, but I never got it.

I had always been good at juggling everything, but, slowly, I started letting all the balls in my life fall down, until I was left holding only the one marked "Addiction." I managed to keep my problems a secret until I had a nearly fatal overdose on Xanax and heroin. My mother was heartbroken and terrified and alone, dealing with a twenty-one-year-old with no sense of accountability. She'd had no previous experience with these types of problems, and no one to talk to. She told me I had two doors to choose from: Door One was to go to rehab, with the full strength of all of my family's support and love and resources; Door Two was to be completely cut off, persona non grata. Like a smart alcoholic, I obviously chose Door One. Mom stood by me and supported me through a twenty-eight-day program that I chose for all the wrong reasons. I had no real intention of staying clean, and I relapsed secretly. I'd gone to rehab for my mother, not for me. The secret to recovery is that it is for people who want it, NOT for people who need it.

I didn't get caught, I didn't have issues with the law, and I didn't OD again. I came clean about my relapse to my mother and my counselor without any burning bush. My impetus was a moment of clarity as I made my way to our appointment, intoxicated and high: I didn't want to live my life like that. Before, I had needed to get sober—for my girlfriend, for my mom, my family—but I hadn't wanted it. Now, for the first time, I wanted to get sober. My mother and my counselor discussed the options, and they decided to send me to treatment.

Still under the influence, I drove away from that meeting to pick up my things and head to the treatment center. On the Bay Bridge, I hit a wall—literally. My car flipped on its side, and I slid across four lanes. I didn't get hurt and I didn't harm anyone else, but it was one last reminder of what drugs and drinking led to.

My mother and counselor reacted immediately. Instead of the planned treatment, within hours they put me in a two-day detox. I hated it. After I had a highly emotional argument with the nurses and my counselor on the second day, my mother and my counselor made the hard decision to put me on a 5150, the California code for a 72-hour lockdown in a psych ward. That made me livid and unreasonable. I demanded that my mom get me out. Call the hospital, call the mayor, I didn't care—she just needed to get me out.

She didn't. She refused. It was the first time that I'd ever faced a punishment that fit my crimes, and it probably saved my life. I finally hit rock bottom in that awful psych ward. I had another moment of perfect clarity: If I didn't get sober, I'd end up here permanently.

There's a saying, "The best thing about rock bottom is that the only place to go is up," which people think means that things are as bad as they can possibly get. "Rock bottom" isn't the lowest point a person can go—no matter how bad things are, objectively, they can always get worse. "Rock bottom" is the lowest point a person actually gets to before they decide to change, when they refuse to go any lower. It's when you can finally see yourself clearly and be honest with yourself without denial or excuses clouding your judgment. I hit rock bottom in my addiction while I still had a family, a home, support, love, and a whole bunch of other things I could have easily lost—but I didn't, because I saw myself clearly and I stopped digging. There are physical rock bottoms as well as spiritual rock bottoms. You don't have to be drinking and drugging to hit a spiritual rock bottom.

I hit rock bottom in my divorce sitting on that airplane when I decided not to read another page. I didn't have to wait for things to be so bad that there was no coming back; I didn't have to drag Nikki and Asher into a pit of misery. I didn't have to stay in my own pit of misery. I needed to put down the shovel and find my way out.

I couldn't imagine leaving Nikki without a support system if Asher ever had problems like that, or any other issues. I couldn't imagine being so alienated that we could not give our son the best of everything we had to offer, all of our love and support, no matter what happened in his life. I wanted to be there to help make Asher face consequences for his actions while he was young, in the hopes we would never have to use tough love as he got older. I didn't want there to be any blind spots he could hide in or holes he could fall down because Nikki and I couldn't communicate or could be easily played off each other. He was only three at the time, but there are countless ways for the best parents in the world to screw up at every age. Giving ourselves a handicap this big wasn't going to make doing our jobs any easier. I wanted to be able to show up for the bad stuff—and I wanted to be able to show up for the good stuff too. I wanted to be able to be in a room with Nikki without awkwardness, to be able to sit together as parents at his school plays or his sport games. I remember to this day how uncomfortable it was when my parents were together for one of our events, and there was no way I was going to put my son through that. I wanted to show up and support our child no matter what happened in our relationship, for his whole life.

Sitting on that plane, I acknowledged that this path was going to lead to a normal, common divorce. Standard divorce is an ugly, combative process that turns an emotionally grueling time—usually that done moment—into something permanent and toxic for everyone it touches, especially the children involved. Divorce as I had known it in my childhood had consequences that far exceeded the legal process. I realized there was no reason for the divorce I was planning to be anything but awful. I wasn't on a path towards justice that would heal my wounds. It wouldn't even necessarily destroy Nikki—and if it did, the fallout from that would be devastating for my son, the person I cared about the most in this world. The only person I was absolutely guaranteed to hurt by going this way was Asher. I had to stop so I didn't repeat my parents' mistakes. I refused to cause that kind of pain in my son's life, which meant I needed to find a different way to do things.

# Sobering Up

Hitting that divorce rock bottom, I was armed mostly with ideas about what I did not want. I did not want a divorce that resembled my parents' divorce. I did not want a high-conflict, public, lengthy court battle. I did not want to punish Nikki, monetarily or otherwise—I was still pissed and I blamed her, but I had realized I couldn't contain the fallout. I did not want to be excluded from my son's life. The only thing I was positive I wanted was to get through this divorce with as little damage to Asher as possible.

I started doing research about alternatives to the standard divorce, and I discovered the collaborative divorce process. The idea was that both of us would sit in a room together with our respective lawyers, and they would mediate the conversation while we tried to collaborate with each other. The isolation of the standard divorce game of telephone, talking through the lawyers to each other, wasn't going to work for me. I knew I wanted to be in the room, so the collaborative method sounded like a step in a better direction.

Cooperating with each other and working together to solve our problems, rather than relying on the lawyers to decide things amongst themselves or throwing ourselves into a courtroom battle, made sense to me. If I wasn't interested in challenging the prenup or any other big fight, I really didn't have a legal issue; I had a relationship issue with legal ramifications. I knew neither of us could "win" our relationship, but we did have problems to solve. When I peeled back the layers of the bullshit ego onion, the facts were simple: Nikki is an awesome mom and a truly great person. I couldn't imagine her taking issue with putting Asher's interests first in the divorce. If her definition of that didn't mean anything like sole custody, hopefully that could mean we'd be on the same side, working together towards the same goal.

The collaborative divorce method also meant we would have more control of the final agreement. There are all sorts of horror stories about lawyers who decide to fight for what they believe is in their client's best interest (regardless of the client's opinion), or judges who give full custody to parents who aren't even requesting it, or award alimony payments that wipe out one party completely. (Not to mention the horror stories about lawyer fees. I knew that if I fought this, we would be giving a fortune to lawyers, money we would much rather spend on Asher.) Nikki and I were already beaten to hell. Starting the next chapter of our lives based on other people's ideas about what would be best for us sounded awful, and I couldn't even guess how it might affect Asher.

I still had some things to figure out before I could really move forward with this process, but it was all a moot point if Nikki and I couldn't talk to each other. We hadn't had a real conversation since I had left my ring behind. I wasn't ready to start, but I had to know if this was an avenue worth exploring.

It all sounded better in theory than a standard divorce, but in order to get good results from it, I needed some time away. By definition, to collaborate with Nikki, I was going to have to work with her, and I was still too angry. I wasn't handing my case off to a lawyer to win, so I needed to have my thoughts in order and know what goals and solutions were acceptable to me. I committed to working through my own issues before having any serious discussions about the divorce.

Alcoholics Anonymous had been the first place I'd learned to be honest with myself and with others around me. It was difficult for me to open up. Even in my initial twenty-eight-day recovery program, I'd been known as the "Everything's Cool Guy." I was always trying to solve everyone else's problems, not share or work on my own. When it was my turn to share, my standard answer was, as you might guess, "Everything is cool."

Before I was twenty-one, as I was being consumed by my addiction, I blamed my parents (and everybody else) for my issues. I was blind to any sense of personal accountability for my actions. Seeking sobriety, I'd needed to learn a lot about boundaries, cause, and effect. A twelve-step program had taught me to be honest and showed me that I was playing a role in every situation where I felt resentment. I learned to take a look at my part in these situations, but I hadn't done that yet with Nikki and our relationship. Looking within for the first time in quite a while, I realized that I needed to work on myself; I needed to see my whole part in this relationship. With the collaborative divorce waiting for me on the other side, I went silent while I attended ninety meetings in ninety days, worked through the steps with my sponsor, and came to realize the role I had played in the end of our marriage.

One of the first things I recognized was how isolated from any of my support networks I had become since Nikki and I had moved to Tampa six years prior. We'd been dating for two years when her parents decided they were going to make the move, and family is everything to Nikki. There was no question in her mind—she was leaving with them, and she asked if I would come with her. I'd been to Miami before and loved it. (Note to the discerning traveler: Tampa is nothing like Miami.) I was working for Nikki's dad, and was completely engulfed in her family. She wouldn't have really known anyone in Tampa besides her family when she arrived, and I didn't want her to be alone. Most of all, I was completely smitten with her. I thought we were going to spend the rest of our lives together—but I wanted to know we were serious and committed to each other before I moved across the country. My marriage proposal had been kind of an ultimatum. It also seemed romantic; Tampa would be the next step of our lives, a very definitive next chapter. We would get married, move, and start a family of our own. The entire relationship felt like a natural progression.

I hadn't really thought about the consequences of moving across the country and what a huge adjustment it would be. I'd grown up in San Francisco; I'd gone to elementary school right in the heart of the city, and then to a high school only four blocks away from that. The biggest move I had ever made was going to college fifteen minutes away from San Francisco in Berkeley, just over the Bay Bridge, and even that had felt like a big deal to me.

My family is massive, very tightknit, and almost all centrally located in San Francisco. My parents and both of my brothers and my sister still live in the city, along with forty or so extended family members who all read like immediate family. To this day, I'm one of about six who have moved away. I didn't do the best job with the move; I'm not great at opening up and sharing my life in person, and I'm awful at doing it over the phone. My family had felt hurt and abandoned after I left for Florida, and I missed them more than I'd admitted to myself.

I had a lot of trouble finding myself in Florida. Honestly, I still struggle with it because it's so different from what I grew up with. The entire state was embroiled in the 2000 Bush election "hanging chad" scandal when we got here. It was a far cry from liberal San Francisco, and, culturally, Tampa seemed like a different planet than my hometown. I felt alienated and isolated and a little terrified of my fellow citizens. Two weeks after we'd completely unpacked, I took a drive to enjoy the beautiful weather (January in Florida certainly has that over northern California). I was listening to music (Beastie Boys or Tribe Called Quest, something along those lines) in my car with the windows down, when a truck pulled up beside me. The driver told me to turn it down. Well, no. What he actually said was, "Turn that n***** shit off." A white dude using racial slurs wasn't something I was used to—or wanted to get used to. The heaviness of the choice to live here hit me hard, and I came home and asked Nikki where the hell she'd moved us to.

That was when the blame game started. I wasn't pissed at Nikki at that point, but I was not joking either. I really blamed Nikki for moving me to Tampa—as though she'd put me in handcuffs and thrown me on the plane. I never considered taking accountability for making the decision for myself. It was a little tiny seed of resentment at first. But because I hadn't done the work I needed to do on myself, as we lived here longer and longer and I experienced more and more of the politics, the culture, and the summers, that seed became a huge flowering grand oak. It drove a wedge in our relationship and, after a while, everything seemed tense—not like there was tension between us, but that as individuals, we had both coiled up.

One of the most significant issues was that when we came to Florida, I'd been completely uprooted from my support system, and I had a hard time finding a local twelve-step program I liked. I was six years sober, and I'd had a big support group in San Francisco. I was used to going to five or six meetings a week, and I had sponsees and a sponsor. When I went to meetings in Tampa, they were different, and I didn't know anybody. I felt like a newcomer again, and I had an ego—I hated feeling like I was new to this. I'd been sober for several years by the time Nikki and I met, and she'd always been very supportive and respectful of it, but in the years leading up to our divorce, I'd all but stopped going to meetings. I'd only go when I went home to San Francisco for a while, and when I did go, I stopped sharing as much. To this day, if I don't go to meetings and participate, I go batshit. It's a very important outlet for me. I go to at least three meetings a week when I'm on my game, and I currently have three sponsees. It was time to admit to myself that, at this point, I wasn't just facing the end of my marriage—I was dealing with untreated alcoholism.

I started attending meetings again, and I relied on them for a lot of my support in both this initial ninety-day period and throughout my entire divorce. It was a healthy, good long-term decision for me. I was able to talk about things that had happened in my marriage and come to terms with them without poisoning my family, friends, and (most importantly) Asher with any painful details. After putting myself back in the middle of the boat for the first ninety days, I realized that it was no different here than anywhere else. All that nonsense of "it being different" had just been my alcoholic mind working overtime to give me an excuse to not go to meetings. The best thing about twelve-step programs is that, no matter what is going on in your life or how many years of sobriety you have, when you reach your hand out for help, there is always someone there to grab it unconditionally. The support and love I got during this time are still overwhelming to think about.

I knew I was relieving my son of an anguish that had hurt me deeply as a boy, and I was laying the groundwork for Nikki and me to be able to include our friends and extended families in our future relationship. I've found that it's often easier to forgive someone who has hurt me than someone who has hurt someone I love, and in the course of any relationship, no matter how good, there are things that happen that reflect poorly on both sides. If I wanted to get serious about putting the past behind me, I knew I couldn't plant these types of landmines in people's memories. If the people who loved me had felt being loyal to me meant being cold to, suspicious of, or hating Nikki, they could never have given us the support that we have built our blended family on. My family and friends came to visit me a lot during the divorce, and I could just lean on them for the love and affection I needed, since I had the group to help me process through the issues.

## Realizing My Role in the Past

Working through the past, I knew I needed to understand what had happened from Nikki's side, what role I had played, and where I was at fault. I had started recognizing that I was accountable as well while I was still holding that lawyer's report on the airplane, which had spurred me back to my twelve-step program. I came to realize that, over time, I'd become isolated and stopped communicating with anyone, including my wife. I had to face reality—I hadn't been sober. I was just abstinent from drugs and alcohol. When I don't do what I need to do in order to live a sober and spiritual life, I basically take a handful of Miracle-Gro and sprinkle it all over my flaws and character defects.

When I first began learning about accountability and struggling to get sober, I was still an angry kid. For years, I had thought I was "drinking at" other people. I blamed everyone else for my addiction issues, particularly my parents. Once I'd learned to face myself, I had realized they weren't anyone's fault but my own. Going through this accountability process again as I examined my marriage, I took a rigorous look back at my own actions, regardless of any of Nikki's. Facing myself, I realized I hadn't been communicative or supportive: I had not been a good husband. I had to come to terms with the fact that it wasn't her fault. Once again, I'd been pointing the finger at other people for my problems, ignoring that it left three fingers pointing right back at me.

I was unhappy in Tampa. I was unhappy in my career. I had gotten depressed and shut myself off from Nikki. I'm a private person, and I can easily get emotionally disconnected, and when things started to go wrong, I had shut down and gone tight-lipped about it. Marriage is tough and overwhelming, and even in healthy ones there will be moments when we feel disconnected, like strangers. The difference is that we talk about it and work it through. Nikki and I didn't. We just let it go, and we drifted farther and farther apart. We had never learned to communicate with each other well, and at a certain point, I stopped communicating at all.

We didn't spend much time together alone as a couple. I was gone a lot of the time; during the day, I'd be in the office or playing golf, and I would be out with the boys at night, or traveling to California to see my family, or going to Vegas to let off steam. Even when we were together, there was always a distance between us. We didn't love to do the same things. Not only were we rarely on the same page, we were rarely even in the same place, and we didn't really want to be. I could count on one hand the trips we went on by ourselves to bond as a couple—and one of those was our honeymoon. When we went on vacation, we'd go with the whole DeBartolo crew, and I'd be playing golf, watching football, and doing things with the guys, while Nikki would be shopping and out with her friends all night. We worked well as part of the larger family; it felt right when we were with her parents and siblings and friends—but not alone, when it was just the two of us. It wasn't that we were angry at each other; it just didn't seem like we knew each other well anymore. Looking within myself, I realized it was another manifestation of the emotional disconnection I'd been feeling—even when I was there, I wasn't. I'd made absolutely. NO effort to do things with Nikki. Everything else in my life had taken priority over our relationship.

When I finally took a step back and got my forty-thousand-foot view again, I could see that our marriage wasn't ending over one action, or one week, or even one year. The bottom line was that it had really ended before it had even started. We'd both walked right through every red light the universe had put in our path. At this point, we'd been getting progressively unhappier for a long time, and we'd spent too much time apart, living separate lives. Our communications had deteriorated so drastically that it was hard to even find our comfortable, friendly zone. I'd gotten depressed and retreated inward and become emotionally absent from my wife. It wasn't Nikki's fault; we'd both played our parts. I needed to hold myself responsible for mine. It wasn't my job to hold her accountable for hers.

Does this seem light on the gory details? Know why? Absolutely none of them mattered. There were no individual incidents that changed everything and listing the details would just inflate them with a false sense of importance. In situations like this, details are used as ammunition, to try to justify hatred and resentment towards the other person. Neither of us were serial killers or puppy kickers, and neither of us were saints. We had ten years of hurtful things we'd done and said. We'd built up countless micro-aggressions and some major hurtful actions against each other, just like every other relationship, good or bad. Despite it all, neither of us were bad people—we were just incompatibly married. We had both felt sad and neglected by the other. We'd been aware that the ways we were acting weren't right, and we'd both dealt with our personal feelings in different ways that ended up hurting the other.

The truth was, we had both checked out from the marriage. I had gone inward, into my mental man cave, and I had closed and locked the door and I hadn't planned to ever let her in again. I was not a happy person. I mean, I'm always pretty grumpy, even when I'm in a good mood, but this was more than grumpy; I was being a miserable human being and an awful husband. Being honest, looking at myself and my behaviors, I wouldn't have wanted to be married to me either. Through this process, I realized that I didn't love myself, and without that, it was absolutely impossible to love someone else. I didn't deserve Nikki, or anyone else, before I could fix these things within me. Feeling bitter about it wouldn't have helped me step up and build a better future for my son. And acting bitter about it, trying to tear Nikki down, would have absolutely destroyed any hope we had to heal.

## Recognizing the Reality of the Present

After accepting my role in our past, I needed to look at the current situation honestly and without malice. When it came down to it, Nikki and I weren't in love with each other the way a romantic couple should be. Many people talk about confusing lust for love; oddly enough, Nikki and I had done the opposite. Our initial romantic passion and sexual energy had fizzled out and worn off pretty quickly. We had been young, and we hadn't really known if that was odd or not. It was an awkward issue to address, so we just hadn't, like many of our other issues. We had become best friends so quickly when we met, and that stayed true for a long time. We loved hanging out; there was lots of laughter and it was always a ton of fun. For many years after we were married, it was like hanging out with my favorite person and the coolest roommate ever. We kept trying to force the romantic spark, clinging to the idea that we were soulmates who wanted to spend our lives with each other, and it just wasn't true. We'd been trying to keep our marriage together for Asher for a while. We had desperately wanted Asher to feel like he had a stable and secure family, which we had equated with a two-parent household. Even while living at a hotel, I had been sneaking back in early every morning to preserve the illusion for Asher that I was still living in the house, that we were a happy family. I'd wake him up and help get him ready, kissing him goodbye before he left for school. I'd known it couldn't last forever, but I'd been scared to put it to an end. Now, I started to realize that it wouldn't take long for this type of pantomime to leave scars of its own on him.

I had never questioned my parents' relationship before their divorce. We'd done a lot together as a family—we took vacations, spent summers up at our ranch in Sonoma, and ate dinner together every night. There was never any yelling or abuse or overt emotional pain. I never thought about their relationship with each other, separate from their roles as parents to us. They were never a demonstrative couple, and I have almost no mental images of them spending time together, just the two of them. In fact, one of my earliest memories was from when I was nine or ten, on our annual family trip to Italy: outside of a beachside hotel in Forte Marmi, my mom and dad kissed each other. My siblings and I marveled—we had never seen them be affectionate towards each other before—and it was obviously unique enough to leave a lasting impression on me.

I hadn't thought about it. Little kids are kind of delightfully self-centered, and I don't think most of them, myself included, spend a lot of time considering their parents as human beings distinct from their roles as Mom and Dad. If someone had ever asked me though, I would have said it was normal. My parents were never very loving towards each other, even when they had been trying to give us the impression that their marriage was healthy and happy, and I'd grown up thinking that's what love and marriage were. On some level, I must have known they were unhappy for longer than they'd shown us, but I'd never truly questioned it, even as an adult. It had taken me a long time to realize that Nikki and I weren't affectionate towards each other anymore, and I'd found it acceptable a lot longer than that. Who knows, maybe that was very "normal," but I was pretty sure it wasn't healthy, and I didn't want Asher growing up to think it was. Part of a parent's job is to model what healthy adult relationships look like, and I recognized that I had brought some of the unhealthy behaviors that I had seen modeled as a child into my marriage. Even if I'd been willing to settle for an unhappy relationship, I couldn't—not unless I was willing to risk seeing Asher settle someday for the same thing. I realized that raising him in the only marriage Nikki and I could mimic wasn't a sacrifice for his sake, even though we'd done it with the best of intentions. It wasn't fair to let him grow up thinking that silent suffering was a good baseline status quo. It was weak parenting. If I was going to show him a marriage, I needed to teach him what being part of a strong, healthy couple means, what he should expect as an adult from himself and his partner, and how wonderful love can be. I realized that having two parents together who were miserable would be worse than having two parents who were apart but happy in their own lives. I could not teach my son what a healthy relationship looked like if I was in an unhealthy one, and I could not teach him to trust my guidance if I was lying to him with my actions.

Staying married this way wasn't an option, and fixing our marriage wasn't an option either. We'd tried therapy multiple times, and it had actually made everything worse. Everything had devolved, and at this point, it felt like having a roommate I was sick of. We'd be waiting for the lease to run out instead of being adults and honestly asking ourselves what we were doing. We had swept things under the rug and picked meaningless fights, and now it was awkward and it wasn't fun for us anymore. We both knew our differences were too big to solve, and we were exposing Asher to unhealthy relationship patterns. It was time to try something new.

I was careful not to try and talk myself into the idea that I didn't love Nikki anymore. It wasn't true and wouldn't have been helpful. Recognizing the type of love I did share with her allowed me to enter our collaboration with the strongest foundation. Looking at our current situation critically, I knew that Nikki and I were not put on this earth to be husband and wife, but to become best friends and bring Asher into the world. We needed a divorce; we were not compatible as a married couple, and we just couldn't provide for each other and didn't love each other the way a husband and wife should. It wasn't anyone's fault—it was just who we were and what reality looked like. The longer we denied that, the more damage we were risking to Asher's future happiness. We needed to acknowledge the love that we did have for each other as friends and admit that it wasn't conducive to being married. We needed to figure out how to harness that into the best relationship we could model honestly for our son.

## Deciding What I Wanted from the Future

Having Asher was the best thing Nikki and I had ever done. We'd been married for two years when we decided to start our family, and Nikki got pregnant very quickly. We were so excited, and there are still so many great memories from that time. I was convinced we were having a girl, and I even told the nurse who was doing the gender sonogram that I didn't know why we were wasting our money just to find out what I already knew. The nurse looked up at me and said, "Congratulations, your girl has a penis." I literally jumped up and down. Even though I was posted by Nikki's head in the delivery room, helping her with her breathing, I almost passed out—the nurses needed to bring me smelling salts.

There never was a more confident pregnant woman than Nikki. Throughout the entire time, she was fearless...until they actually handed her the baby. There is one picture of her in that delivery room that perfectly captured how scared she suddenly was. She'd never been around babies before, and Asher was a few months old by the time I convinced her she wasn't going to break him.

My mom loves babies. Walking down the street, she'll randomly approach parents and their youngest children, and she usually ends up holding the babies and making them laugh. It's pretty incredible to behold—I jokingly call her the baby whisperer. Some of that must have rubbed off on me, because I've always been comfortable around babies. I have younger siblings and half siblings, so I also had some practical experience (there are a lot of pictures of me holding my baby sister, Liza, like a wizened, five-year-old pro). I was able to put my skills to good use with Asher, and Nikki and I worked through her fears together. It was probably the closest we've ever been.

I might have had a head start, but once she got her sea-legs, Nikki blew me out of the water. She has always been very organized and generous, and she's a great friend who loves to take care of people. Everyone else was a dress rehearsal, though—Nikki's starring role is being a mom. My mother and Nikki share several incredible traits; they are, in many ways, very similar women—strong, sensitive, and dedicated to their children above all other things. Although the strong bond between Nikki and me after Asher's birth did not make everything right in our marriage, I have always and will always respect Nikki as a mother. I've never once doubted her commitment to our son. I knew

I could trust her to always put his happiness first, and I knew she felt the same way towards me as a father. It was the solid foundation that we built our future on.

There was one good thing that came out of my parents' divorce, and it was something I recognized I needed to focus on during my own. My father and I share certain traits, good and bad. My ability to be cool in any crisis is all him, but so are some of the difficulties I have expressing my emotions and communicating. After he moved out, I was surprised to find it didn't feel like a huge change. He had been home with us every night before, but I realized I'd never felt like he was completely emotionally checked in. Having partial custody of his kids brought us all together in so many ways—some that I don't think any of us had known we'd been missing, and some that I'm still discovering today. He was forced to stay more present and focused by certain things that had always been my mother's exclusive domain, like preparing dinners and reading bedtime stories to my younger siblings and helping us get homework done. He started emphasizing making some good, big memories with us. I remember when he showed up in a rented Ferrari right after the divorce, and we drove up the coast to Carmel for the day, just to enjoy being together. The thing that really sticks out to me now, though, is that every morning he drove the ten blocks to my mother's house to pick us up and take us to school. It was only a ten-minute drive, and it never seemed like a big deal. It took having a teenager myself to realize how much you can learn about your kids in small ways each day; those ten minutes stack up. The fact that he chose to be involved this way, doing something I completely took for granted at the time, means everything to me now.

I was a good father; I had been a really good father when Asher was very young, but the problems I'd had with emotional distance had touched all my relationships. I knew I wanted to be even more involved in Asher's life, and I followed my dad's lead. Divorce helped us both become much more hands-on—much better fathers.

I knew that nothing mattered more to Nikki and me than our son's happiness, health, and well-being, and that we'd both do anything to make sure the divorce didn't hurt him. When we started working together on the divorce and our plans for the future, Asher had to come first; it couldn't be just lip service and it couldn't turn into best intentions. I wanted for every decision we made to build towards Asher's life in a positive way. I wanted that single principle to cover absolutely every aspect of our lives—all the work and healing we needed to do, and every relationship we needed to build. I wanted us both to genuinely value whatever sacrifices that would entail. If I could have a future where Nikki and I both committed everything to making Asher's life the everything it could be, I thought—I hoped—I could deal with anything else.

Before I brought that determination back to the table and started the conversation, I found out Nikki was spending time with someone we'd both known very well. It was very difficult to know there was a man around my soon-to-be ex-wife and around my son, and it was painful to realize it was someone I'd considered a friend. I was incredibly hurt. The two big red buttons that make divorces go bad are romance and finance, and this one jammed hard on the romance button. It felt like a test to my commitment: One way or the other, I wouldn't have to wonder whether I could really put Asher ahead of my personal feelings.

In the end, I worked through the issue pretty quickly. I knew I had to let go of my ego and insecurities to create the best atmosphere for my son to thrive. I realized that both Nikki and I were going to see other people. I was going to make sure that I only brought people into Asher's life who could love and care for him as much as Nikki and I did, and I had to trust Nikki to do the same. If this man met that criteria, it didn't matter if he was my brother or best friend or a perfect stranger—I owed him gratitude, not jealousy.

The work I had done in those ninety days gave me enough insight to move forward and collaborate. I knew what I wanted from the divorce and I had my goals. Asher's future mattered to me more than anything else, and I could build from there. From my forty-thousand-foot view, I could see it was time for the next step—sitting down with Nikki and making amends. I was spiritually sound and fit, ready to get the legal portion of the divorce finished and start doing the work to rebuild our family. Holding myself accountable and working on my relationships with my son and family started here, but I was far from finished. I had known going in that this break couldn't last forever. I couldn't wait until I was a perfect person to come back and start working on the future. This wasn't ever going to be the perfect divorce, but I already had a lot of hope it could be a happy divorce—and happiness means constant growth.

I picked up the phone and hit the number that still occupied the top spot in my most frequent call list. Oddly enough, I felt completely calm and collected when Nikki picked up. Her neutral "hello" solidified my certainty that, even with no roadmap ahead, I was on the right path.

"Hi, Nikki…can we meet?"

We sat in silence for only a few seconds. I thought about the expression I was sure she was making at that very moment, her thoughtfulness, the care she took when making decisions.

"Okay," she said softly. "When? Where? Just us, or…?"

Oh man, I thought, laughing at myself. It had been so long since I'd asked someone out on a date that I'd made a rookie mistake—I didn't have a plan beyond getting the "yes."

Tomorrow? Next week? The momentum was good, though, I didn't want to lose that. Dinner? Too formal.

"No, just us. Do you have time for coffee, like, now? We can meet at the Starbucks right around the corner from the house."

"Give me an hour?"

"Sure, I'll meet you there."

I hung up the phone and paced for a while before heading out for the most nerve-wracking coffee date of my life.

# Nikki

I hung up the phone and sat for a moment, trying to collect my thoughts. I'm a planner, an organizer, someone who likes to know the lay of the land before I walk into a meeting. If I had a month, though, I wouldn't have been able to properly prepare for this one. I knew I'd done a lot of soul searching since finding that abandoned wedding band, but I had no idea where Ben's thoughts were, who he had become. I knew we were both in the middle of transformations and that, in some ways, we were meeting up as completely new people. I didn't know what to expect when I walked into that coffee shop.

I asked Lisa to watch Asher while I took care of something. My expression must have betrayed the uncertainty roiling inside of me because, for once, she didn't press for details, and I didn't offer any.

I drove to the Starbucks on autopilot, pulled into a parking space next to Ben's SUV, turned off the car, and just sat for a moment. I took my keys out of the ignition and then put them back in.

Maybe I should park on the other side of the lot, in case walking out together would be awkward? Maybe I should just leave?

I shook myself off and wondered if Ben was watching me. I turned to look inside the coffee shop, but the sun was behind me, bouncing off the windows and making them into mirrors.

Deep breath, Nikki, I coached myself. If worse turns to worst, you can always just leave.

I stepped out onto the pavement and headed towards the storefront, counting my steps for balance.

The store was pleasantly busy and humming—enough people that it didn't feel like I'd just entered a saloon for a Wild West-style shootout, but not so many that I worried about sharing a table (or a divorce) with strangers. Ben was already seated at a table to my left with just two cups in front of him—no paperwork, no phone, nothing else.

"Tall non-fat cappuccino?" he asked as I approached.

I gave him a grateful half-smile in acknowledgment. Sure, I was pleased he remembered my drink order, but I wasn't going to fall into a swoon over a cup of coffee.

I studied him out of the corner of my eye as I arranged my purse on the back of the chair and sat down. Sitting across from him, alone together for the first time in what felt like forever, was nerve-wracking. Something was different about him. His arms, usually crossed, hung by his sides. His foot jiggled like an ad for restless leg syndrome medication. He seemed anxious, but less tense than he'd been for some time.

When he opened his mouth, I stopped breathing, completely uncertain what was coming next.

"Nikki, I'm sorry."

I exhaled, momentarily dumbfounded. I never would have guessed that would be Ben's opening line. As I tell people now, it was the first and last time I've ever heard him apologize for anything!

He kept going; he apologized for the part he'd played in the collapse of our marriage, and he told me he loved me. And then he waited for my response.

A weight lifted off my shoulders. Yes, I could forgive him, and yes, I could forgive myself. I apologized for my portion and told him I loved him too.

We both smiled, and then Ben asked me his first question, making clear what mattered to him most: "Do you have any problem with joint custody?"

When I said no, he told me that we could work out everything else.

Sitting in that coffee shop that day, we made a vow and a commitment to put Asher first, no matter what happened in the whole process. Whatever decisions we had to make, we had to ask ourselves how they would affect Asher. It was the primary lens, the single platform, from which we would build everything. We had our mission and our first principle. Knowing our focus, everything was clear and the path forward was visible. From that moment on, the most complicated process that anyone ever has to go through was so easy for us. We walked away that day as a team—still badly banged up, but no longer quite so broken.

We hashed out all of our divorce plans over the course of a few more coffee dates. We always met at the same Starbucks—actually, we always met at the same table. Ben would have his venti black coffee and my tall non-fat cappuccino ready and waiting, so we could dive straight into the important stuff. We carefully framed every topic we discussed through that one question: What's best for Asher? It took on a variety of forms—What divorce method will be the least difficult for Asher? What custody arrangement will make Asher the happiest? What financial arrangement will provide best for Asher? What interpersonal relationship do we need to build to create the healthiest atmosphere for Asher? The answers to those questions were our answers, and the highest truth we needed.

What method of divorce is going to be the least difficult on Asher? We had agreed to a collaborative divorce, but we took it a step further than most people. I don't think there's a name for the divorce method we used. Essentially, we agreed to negotiate the legal terms of our divorce during our coffee shop dates together, without even our lawyers present to mediate. We knew we could seek out the help of whatever professional legal representation, arbiters, mediators, and negotiators we felt we needed, but first we wanted to try and figure out what was best for us without influence. We knew we wanted to get through the actual legal divorce process in whatever way would be the fastest, while minimizing the stress between us, that could create the best foundation for our future. Any time we spent dragging it out was time we were stealing from Asher, and he needed us. Any animosity we created would make it harder for us to be civil in front of Asher, and we owed him our healthiest possible relationship. Any decisions made by other people—well, how could we even know what type of foundation that would leave us? For Asher's sake, we needed to be in control of the process, so we could make every choice, small through large, in his best interest.

Since we shared such a strong mutual goal, we knew we didn't need to fight each other. The idea of being adversaries, fighting across a courtroom, when we were both trying to "win" the same thing, made no sense.

Our entire agreement started with our mutual commitment to joint custody; we knew that Asher needed us both to be equally engaged in his life. Our dedication to sharing our time with him 50/50 has shaped our family and our lives in unique ways, and it's been one of the highlights of building our happy divorce. During these initial coffee shop talks, the logistics of our custody arrangement seemed relatively easy. We agreed to split the time evenly, week-by-week, and I would have Thanksgivings with Asher on odd years and Christmases on even years, while Ben got the even Thanksgivings and odd Christmases.

While we were correct that evenly split custody was the best solution for Asher, we realized along the way that we needed to modify the weekly trade—actually, we needed to pretty continually modify it. Between work and travel, Ben and I both have complicated schedules. The strict arrangements common to a typical divorce (where one parent has custody every weekend, or every other Wednesday, for example) wouldn't have worked for any of us. If Ben or I needed to be out of town during our custody week, were we supposed to tell Asher he just wouldn't be able to see one of us for three weeks? We did not want to use custody as a weapon to get back at the other person. We realized that we were more concerned with doing the best thing for Asher than owning designated timeslots, so we valued making sure our custody remained evenly split, even if it made the logistics more complicated. We both agreed that we were flexible to shift scheduling, so that Asher never had to sacrifice any of his time with either of us. We started sitting down and creating our co-parenting calendar each month, continually working together to make sure we never lost sight of Asher's needs, even in our most hectic months.

Mapping custody for summer vacations was particularly crazy. During the school year, Ben and I live in the same town, so it's easy for Asher to go back and forth between his two houses, but he becomes a world-class traveler when school lets out. Last year, Asher went to Hawaii with Ben's family, then he came to stay with me in California (I spend a large portion of the summer in Los Angeles with my mother and sisters). A little later, Ben and his family joined us in L.A., and we all went to Montana together. This year Asher left Montana with Ben, and they spent ten days having adventures in the RV before Asher met me at home in Tampa. We are careful to make sure custody is still split equitably, but Asher usually ends up staying longer with each of us (usually about two weeks) before switching off, so that he has time to enjoy all the activities. Back in Florida in the fall, though, he usually stays in each house for three or four nights. Routinely spending a week apart from either Ben or me, as we'd originally planned in the coffee shop meetings, ended up being too much for Asher. At his request, we later agreed that shortening each visitation period during the school year was a much better plan.

Money is always an awkward topic, even at the best of times, and finances are usually one of the most divisive things about a divorce. No matter how much or little money there is, most couples have collected things together. People who are splitting finances and assets are thrown into a competitive situation by default. Even if they are trying to be fair or generous, they are staring down at resources they've had access to and wondering what life will be like without them. I was only thirty-three, and Ben was thirty-six, but we had considerable and complicated assets—far more complicated than the majority of couples facing divorce. Our mutual goal, though, clarified everything, even the financial settlement.

We had signed a prenuptial agreement, but those are contested in court all the time. Some couples spend years arguing about every contingency. By the standard logic, a couple trying to reach a rational and mature settlement would rely solely on the agreement—that was fair, right? This legal document had been drawn up in case we were ever faced with exactly the situation we were in.

However, when we ran the question through our lens (what financial settlement is going to be best for Asher?), it gave us a whole different perspective. Our agreement had addressed the possibility of children, of course—it covered everything, hypothetically. Looking at the documents we'd signed years earlier, we realized how different everything looked now that it was real. We knew more about ourselves, our lives, and most importantly, our son. Asher wasn't just a future possibility anymore, like he had been when we made this agreement. When we put this together, we had different goals and priorities than we did now. Our priority now was our son, and a successful financial settlement couldn't be measured by how fair it was to each other, or whether it paid out justice for anything that had gone wrong between us. The right financial settlement for us was the one that would allow us to make the best life for our son, so we worked on a new one.

We created the settlement that ensured the healthiest atmosphere for Asher, regardless of whose house he was staying in at any given moment. We made sure Asher would never want for anything or see either of us struggling. We didn't need a fair settlement; we needed to provide for each other, like the family we would always be.

Even divisions that seemed like they wouldn't affect Asher directly made perfect sense once we ran them through our lens. We realized that everything we decided on would affect his well-being in some way. We owned several businesses together, including a jewelry business and a record label. What division would be best for Asher? Well, Ben and I had separate interests, and we had each put more work into different businesses. What was best for Asher was that Ben and I treated each other as the friends/family he needed us to be—careful, considerate, respectful, kind, generous, and loving. Asher's interests were best served by the two of us avoiding bitterness and conflict-for-the-sake-of-conflict. He was also owed being able to watch both of his parents engaging in things they were passionate about. If, for example, Ben had taken the jewelry business, I would have been crushed and he would have been stressed. I'd put so much of myself into that, and he wouldn't have enjoyed the work involved. We were able to look at our assets and divide them according to our interest and sweat equity. I got the jewelry company, and Ben loves music, so he got the record label, and we worked our way from there. Going down the list became so much easier after we framed it properly with our goal in mind.

## Forgiving Each Other

If we were forced to boil down what we've learned in the process of building our post-divorce relationship to one bullet point, it would be that nothing was more important than our son. If we got two, though, the second one is an easy choice: it's all about forgiveness.

When people ask how we were able to immediately start liking one another again, we used to laugh and tell them we faked it until we made it. Really, though, "faked" isn't the right word. Yes, sometimes our shared smiles were a little brittle, especially when we were just starting to heal. There's something to the observation that every marriage has phases when it's only held it together with sex and good manners; during the divorce, Ben and I were down to just good manners, so they counted for a lot. We didn't have to pretend to love each other, though; we had to find the best ways to express our love, as badly as we had mangled it, and rebuild our trust in each other. We put our egos aside when we were together and stepped away for a breather if we ever felt the need to be cutting. We worked on learning how to establish a healthy relationship based on our mutual goal. It started with the coffee shop meetings, where we built the foundation for starting our next chapter after the divorce, and the most important feature of our relationship today.

Once again, it all came down to our most important question: What's best for Asher? We both wanted a happy and emotionally healthy kid, and we were willing to do anything in our power to make that happen. If the best way to do that is to be as happy and emotionally healthy ourselves as possible, okay! It's not as dramatic as throwing ourselves to the sharks or walking over hot coals, true. Sometimes sacrifice doesn't have to suck. Ben and I have made a ton of sacrifices since we got divorced—way more than either of us made while we were married—and the vast majority of them have been, actually, pretty nice in both the short- and long-term. The sacrifices we've chosen have made us happier, healthier people than when we were acting defensively, trying to guard ourselves from whatever hurt we saw coming.

# Redefining Roles

We believe that people are put in our lives for certain reasons; Ben and I were put on this earth to be best friends, not husband and wife. Okay, so we'd gotten it wrong—how many people choose all their lifelong roles perfectly in their twenties? How long did we need to beat ourselves up for it? Ten years? Twenty? The rest of our lives? It seemed like a pretty significant time and energy commitment that we could put towards the well-being of our son instead.

Deep down, we already knew we shouldn't be married before anything even came to a head. Nothing we'd done to each other in those last days would have been hurtful if we'd already been divorced, if we'd been friends or siblings or in any other type of relationship. We might have had a spat over a few of them, but most of them would have been just water under the bridge—no big deal. What had been hurt the worst were our egos, because we had to admit we'd been wrong, and the worst thing we'd done to each other was taking away the hope we'd be clinging to. Time could heal all that.

It didn't happen immediately, and we knew we were going to have to work our way back to being best friends. We couldn't force it, and we didn't need to. Our primary roles to each other now didn't rely on that, though. We'd become parents first and spouses a distant second the moment Asher was born. The jobs that mattered were being Mom and Dad, and respecting and supporting each other as co parents. We needed to jettison whatever baggage was left from our marriage quickly so that we could perform even better in our roles as parents.

# Pettiness, Bitterness, and Grudges

Initially, Ben's ego was probably even more bruised than mine (not that it was a competition). The fact that he was the one who initiated the coffee shop meeting to discuss collaborating on the divorce, moving forward, and healing was a big deal to me. Ben had extended that olive branch, and I knew I needed to step up to meet him.

Of course, we were still both hurt. We were dealing with wounded pride and feelings of failure, but no amount of spite or bitterness was going help fix any of that or heal either of us. Being petty doesn't heal anyone. It might have felt good for a moment to hurt Ben on purpose, or to convince people to be on "my" side, but I couldn't build a healthy life that way for myself, and certainly not one for Asher.

Ben is great at projecting outward cool when he's broken up inside—it's one of his superpowers. During the divorce and afterwards, he seemed extremely, almost frighteningly together, and it helped assure me that we were going to be able to do this, to make this work. As for me, I can only hold a grudge when someone hurts the people I love. Ben and I were doing the opposite; we were planning on how to make Asher's life more amazing with every conversation. Refusing to give my best to each one of those conversations and interactions would have been the same as choosing to take something important away from my son.

I think most people expected us to be in the fetal position in the corner, at least for a minute. We definitely had our moments of shock and disbelief, and it's not like we were thrilled. We had all the appropriate emotions, but we never let in vengeance, hate, negativity, or spite. We were extremely aware that the situation we were working on would be influenced by our emotions, and anything bad or lazy we let touch it would ultimately affect Asher, and we stayed very mindful of that. Asher gave us the strength to get through this in the best ways possible. We loved him more than enough to make our decisions and base our actions on what was best for him.

Ben and I both know that our story and accomplishments rely heavily on forgiveness and understanding, and that's something many people struggle with. We're exceptionally fortunate that neither of us is big on holding grudges, but we also know that those are choices. It can be really, really hard to not choose pettiness. A lot of people don't think they can work past their initial pain, and they lash out before they can see the bigger picture. We're not claiming a lack of personality flaws between us, but we don't stock up the pettiness department. We're experts on how to forgive and not cast a lot of judgment because we know how much we've personally benefited from people extending those gifts to us. We understand we're both doing the best we can, but that we're going to come up short and make mistakes sometimes, and we're not going to hold that against each other. It's not that we don't hold each other to very high standards; we've just had to brush ourselves off too many times to blame anyone for tripping. Our modern family takes a lot of work, and if each one of us doesn't hold the others accountable, it won't work. We make mistakes all the time—we just don't double down on those mistakes by holding grudges. We forgive each other and try harder. Striving for perfection or retribution clearly makes a lot of people very unhappy during their divorces and at every other juncture. Ben and I realize that we get to make choices all the time between being right and being happy. Even if we weren't prioritizing our son, I'd like to think we would still have chosen happiness.

## No Monsters Here

Ben and I were both absolutely heartbroken when we split up. Each of us had thought we'd married a good person. Were we wrong? The natural default (as much lip service as we can pay to the idea that two good people can just not be good together) is to assume there is a "good guy" and a "bad guy" in a split. There was no real "bad guy" between us; we were just getting increasingly toxic towards each other the longer we were together.

If either of us had ever been abusive to our child, if we had been physically abusive to each other, or if we had been emotionally abusive in serious, threatening ways, we could not have built the life we have today. Nothing matters to either of us more than our son, and neither one of us would have kept a relationship going in any form with a person who was bad for Asher. Ben and I agree those are big things, and we're grateful we didn't have to deal with any of that. There are also little things, those red buttons of finance and romance, which feel like the end of the world. People who are hurt label each other as complete monsters for giving awful birthday presents, or not helping around the house, or watching sports too often, falling in love with someone else, or forgetting Valentine's Day. Ben and I agreed that being disappointed, being hurt, or disagreeing when the rules of the game change were all fine reasons to end our marriage, but not great reasons to carry around the baggage for decades or try to ever keep Asher away from each other.

The bottom line was that we were both loving, caring parents and good people. We didn't mislabel each other when we were hurt. It would have only ultimately hurt our son. It would have been shortsighted to hate each other forever; any hateful feelings we had towards each other were symptoms of our bad marriage, not proof we were bad people. It's so much harder to hate someone than to love and accept them, and we knew the more time we spent hating each other, the less time we had for our son and to heal ourselves and him and build something better. At one point, every married couple promised to try their hardest to build a life together. For Ben and me, that's a promise we wanted to keep, even though we couldn't stay married. Hatred would have clouded our vision for Asher, and that just wasn't acceptable.

It is natural to be afraid of the dark. We are all threatened by what we cannot see and comprehend. I grew up dreaming about my fairytale wedding, my princess gown; I could have described it all in detail by the time I was five. I grew up in the stability of my parents' marriage, watching them work through everything life threw at them. I did not grow up daydreaming about my divorce—and I don't think many people do. Divorce is a pitch-black unknown for so many of us, and people who are threatened and afraid act on defensive mechanisms. At the first coffee shop meeting, Ben and I made so many crucial decisions and distinctions that helped us move forward and build everything we have today. The most important thing we did, though, was come up with a vision we could share for our divorce. Our vision was specific enough to give us hope, but broad enough to cover the legal process and the collaborative steps we would need to take to build our post-divorce family. When we finally finished signing the divorce papers, it was a bittersweet victory, but it was a victory  the first big measurable one we had achieved together, as a team, towards this new life. Our choice to commit to the well-being of our son was the flashlight we needed to navigate through the darkness; it allowed us to pick up, step over, and move around every obstacle we would face.

# Ben

There wasn't a lot of information available on collaborative divorce when Nikki and I went through ours. Now, twelve years later, there are more books and better programs to train professionals in the industry, and there are some resources out there for people looking for alternative paths to take in their own divorces. It's still much more difficult to find solid advice on the process than we would hope, based on our own incredible experience with it. Wading through the platitudes and high-level explanations of the process that a Google search turns up is more confusing than helpful to me—and I've already been through one. I can't imagine what it must be like for someone new to the idea, trying to get clear answers in the middle of processing the tough emotions that come with a relationship ending.

It's hard to put together something like a collaborative divorce checklist that would cover everything for everyone. They aren't one size-fits-all; they're custom-built, and I suspect that if we asked a dozen different couples who have gone through a collaborative divorce, we'd hear about a dozen different methods and results.

Nikki and I chose what we were going to make of it. If we'd put less work in, we still would've had a better experience and outcome than we'd have gotten from a standard divorce, but we wouldn't have built the foundation for our post-divorce family. Our choices didn't just amount to not going to court or not being cruel to each other—we worked hard and truly collaborated to make our divorce goal-oriented. Centering the agreements and legal documentation around "What's best for Asher?" minimized our pain and helped us build new lives as seamlessly as possible. We didn't have to take time to regroup and refocus after the divorce, because we made it a vital part of our path forward.

Making our dedication to Asher the founding principle for our post-divorce family worked because it was not complicated. We didn't need to weigh our options or rationalize it. We were already fully focused on his well-being, and it wasn't in competition with anything else. We made it very clear it wasn't about us; our emotions and our feelings and our egos were beside the point, and we took them completely out of the equation. Absolutely everything was about Asher's well-being and what was best for him and to make sure he wasn't emotionally ruined because of a decision he had absolutely nothing to do with. Working together to achieve the goal we both wanted more than anything in the world helped us put everything else into perspective during the divorce and during the hardest early days of building our blended family—and it still helps us today. We knew from the beginning that we couldn't gain anything from bad behavior or taking shortcuts or half-assing our efforts that would be worth jeopardizing Asher's happiness, and we were clear that was what was at stake. Shaping our divorce together still wasn't fun, but it wasn't crushing either, and it taught us new skills. Even though we were still hurting, we came away from the legal process proud of our teamwork and accomplishments. We didn't have to walk into meetings already on the defensive and we never had to dread awful surprises, so we used that time and emotional energy to continue growing as people and parents. In comparison, the interactions we had with the standard divorce industry were bleak, damaging, and expensive.

Before we started considering alternatives, finding my first, divisive attorney wasn't an accident—it had been my goal. I'd searched thoroughly for the dirtiest fighter to "win" my divorce. I'd ended up hiring the first name my very successful attorney friend had given me when I'd asked for the best attack dog he knew. I'd been surprised, though, how reluctant my friend had been to give me the recommendation. He'd tried to talk me out of anything litigious, suggesting a peaceful solution instead. I had been too pissed and certain I'd win to take the advice right away, but it had gnawed away at a corner of my brain. After my revelation on the plane, I realized my friend hadn't been trying to talk me out of it because he thought I'd lose—he'd been afraid of what would happen if I "won." He was right: I hadn't considered what the awful ramifications of "winning" would have been. I was unable to imagine what my long-term goals and desires were, as I had been reacting to temporary feelings of rage driven by my ego.

Standard divorces are legal matters, and our legal system is based on retributive justice—the idea that a criminal, a wrongdoer, needs to be punished. A court case would have established either Nikki or me as the "wrongdoer" (and the "winner" as the victim). We had both wronged each other at times—not in any sort of crazy criminal ways, but we had both done wrong. That didn't make either of us a wrongdoer, and applying those labels to our relationship would've resulted in dire consequences. They would have changed the ways we felt about ourselves and each other, shaped what was possible and where the story could go. Most stories have a villain, they have a good guy and a bad guy, but not this one—ours didn't ever need one. For me, "winning" in the courtroom would have created Nikki-the-wrongdoer and Ben-the-victim. Nikki-the-wrongdoer might have felt bad about herself, or she might have been angry that she'd been blamed for everything. This villain identity would have lived on long after our time in court was over and the divorce was finalized. There are many ways people react to being cast as villains, none of which would have helped her or Asher heal after the divorce. Ben-the-victim would never have felt accountable. I would have missed the opportunity to realize how depressed I'd gotten and make myself and my life better. I would have never had the impetus to look at my part in the marriage, forgive Nikki, and let go of my anger. It would have been impossible to build the incredible family we have today. A court case would have been a permanent record casting the things we'd done as if they were who we were. Instead of "wrongdoer" and "victim," the collaborative process let us both be who we truly were: People who'd made mistakes. That was familiar territory because, shockingly enough, neither of us had made it into our thirties without making a mistake before. We'd both had a 100 percent success rate for living through those prior mistakes, and cast in that light, we'd felt pretty sure we could keep that streak going. We gave ourselves the space to acknowledge the things we'd done, fix what could be fixed, forgive everything, and move on.

It didn't make sense for the wrongs we'd done to each other to define our divorce, because they hadn't defined our marriage. They were just symptoms of the actual problem, which was that we simply weren't compatible in a romantic relationship. Pitting ourselves against each other as adversaries, spending months or years trying to punish each other for ultimately inconsequential wrongs, wouldn't have even addressed the real issue. If nothing had mattered more to us than destroying each other, if we'd been willing to sacrifice everything— our health, sanity, our child, and any sense of perspective—one of us might have gotten "justice," but that would have been an awful victory for everyone involved except the lawyers and the system. The collaborative divorce freed us from the labels that didn't work (husband and wife) without imposing equally ill-fitting new ones (wrongdoer and victim), giving us the chance to build a healthy environment for Asher afterwards as the best versions of ourselves.

The initial process the shark attorney led me through didn't encourage me to take a step back and think rationally about what would be best for me and for my family. When I'd started speaking with him, I'd wanted payback, literally, for all my anger and pain. That worked fine for him; on our first call, he'd only really wanted details about our marital financial arrangements. He must have liked what he heard, because when I finished, he was confident that he— we—could "win." He'd nurtured my anger and sense of injustice and offered to legitimize them. If I hadn't made a breakthrough on my own, I would have committed to turning that difficult emotional moment into lifelong legal ramifications. Litigious divorce attorneys prop up those temporary feelings, but it's not that lawyers are bad people; they're just doing the job they've been hired for, and it's not a heartwarming humanitarian effort. The majority of divorces still play out in the courtroom because there's no immediate reason for people to search for alternatives; they're already being served by the system built around the strong emotions they're feeling.

When the shark had talked about driving an eighteen-wheeler through the prenup, all I heard was that I'd be getting my cold revenge. To this day, Nikki still scoffs and says that never would have happened; her lawyers would have killed it. Nikki's legal team wasn't sitting in the dark, hoping I would come to my senses; they were gearing up for a fight too, and like all talented litigators, they would have been well-equipped for the confrontation. Standard divorce attorneys stoke and maintain emotional fires for many reasons, including their bottom lines. They profit from keeping clients angry and irrational and fighting for as long as possible. They get paid handsomely and by the hour, and the more conflict they can create, the more money they'll make. In any standard divorce, the attorneys on both sides have equal incentive to drag everything out, and once the case is in their hands, the client doesn't have complete control over when they decide to stop fighting. The bills can add up quickly, and it seems like the rule, not the exception, for divorce costs to balloon beyond any client's wildest dreams.

I paid a ten-thousand-dollar retainer to the shark to take my case, and when Nikki and I decided on a collaborative divorce, I asked him to return the portion that hadn't been used. Conveniently, there was nothing left on it—and he'd done nothing more than review my prenup and write that twenty-five-page report. Looking back on it, that was the best ten-thousand dollars I've ever spent in my life. If I had never gotten that drastic and intense report, if I had never been smacked in the face with how awful the path I was taking us all down could be, things might have ended very differently. Spending that money so that I could end up limiting the emotional cost to Asher was well worth it, and it was definitely our primary motivation for changing direction. Still, avoiding the final price tag of an entire litigious standard divorce with the shark (to say nothing of Nikki's legal fees—and the judge would have likely stuck one of us with the bill for both sides) was a nice bonus. In comparison, my bill from my collaborative attorney was a pleasant surprise for me. After everything was said and done, I owed her only a few thousand dollars, less than a third of what I'd paid for a single report from the shark. Nikki's lawyer drafted the final documents, so her bill was probably higher, but it still could not have compared to what it would have cost to litigate.

Stepping back and apologizing to each other changed the course of our lives and saved us a lot of time and money that we were able to put towards making sure our son was healthy and happy instead. We couldn't be married, and that was hard enough; destroying our kid and families and flinging cash at lawyers indiscriminately would have just layered bad decisions on top of the sadness. The collaborative divorce allowed us to start healing and helped us iron out some of our issues in ways that were actively beneficial for our son and our future.

It cost so much less—in every way.

I barely spoke with my attorney in the collaborative process, and I don't think she was nearly as pleased as I was with the paltry number of billable hours she accrued. By the time I involved her in anything, Nikki and I had already decided what was best for our family over the course of our coffee shop dates. I was taught that the business people should make the business decisions, not lawyers, and Nikki and I were business partners in these divorce proceedings. The lawyers were just there to write up and review the terms, not dictate them to us. We worked through notoriously acrimonious legal issues with relative ease because, for us, these were just the forms. The real hard work was going to be making the best life for Asher, and we needed to slog through this paperwork so we could focus our attention on that. Our divorce wasn't an exciting, dramatic battle, or even the end of our lives together. These were the formalities to close this chapter and move on, together, to the next.

## Mediator and Marriage Counselors

In addition to having one collaborative attorney each, Nikki and I hired two other professionals, although neither of them ended up being necessary. We met with a mediator during the settlement, who was authorized to make final decisions for us if there was anything we couldn't resolve between ourselves. We've never used her—we've never even come close to needing her. We also met with another person to help us map out custody, but neither of us fought for more than the even split we'd agreed on in the coffee shop. Nikki and I walked into our meetings with a holistic view for our family's future, so we were fortunate enough to not require their advice. I was still glad the options existed, just in case; they were precision instruments, trained to be very good at their portion of the job. At the same time,

I wouldn't want a dentist to do a full-body physical; I would want advice from a doctor trained to look at the whole picture, and the fact that Nikki and I couldn't find a good divorce doctor to help us develop our overall plan surprised us.

Nikki and I visited marriage counselors while we were still trying to avoid divorce, and the experiences ranged from "not helpful" to "actively inflicting more damage." One of the most memorable debacles took place after I'd moved out, when I was still sneaking in every morning to help get Asher off to school. We'd thought we were really lucky to score an appointment with a therapist in Boston who had written a popular book on relationships. We'd both known he wouldn't magically solve our problems, but we'd hoped he could point us in the right direction and give us some tools to start working everything through.

The appointment was a complete disaster. The doctor decided he disliked Nikki before she even opened her mouth, and he was ridiculously hostile towards her. He went so far as to call her spoiled and a brat. Every time I left the room, he would challenge her and taunt her to "come clean." Between how combative he was and the wedges he tried to jam in all over the place, we walked out of his office in worse shape than when we had arrived. His fees weren't cheap, and we wondered why we spent so much money to be insulted by this jerk.

Our first exposure to the divorce therapy industry alerted us to how bizarrely divisive it could be, and our last session had all the charm of, well, a state-sponsored class. People seeking a divorce in Florida with children under the age of eighteen have to take a four-hour course before they can finish filing. Theoretically, it should have been awesome and helpful for Nikki and me. It's supposed to teach parents how to stabilize the situation for the benefit of the children and how to get through everything with as little wear and tear on the family as possible. In reality, the one that we attended took an extremely adversarial approach. Once again, we were stuck in a room with a professional who kept insisting we shouldn't be friends with our children. To switch it up, I was the one that elicited the negative reaction this time. One or two hours of being demeaned by a woman who didn't know us or care about our family was fun, but once the thrill wore off, I spoke up (okay, I blew up, but just a little). Rather than handle my outburst professionally, she smirked at me and said, "No wonder you're here." It seemed both cruel and shortsighted, especially since Nikki and I were the only people there who'd chosen to take the class together as a couple. We've never pretended we're perfect, but we'd been as conscientious as possible about our divorce, so being mocked by a mental health practitioner was a kick in the teeth.

In these brief "therapeutic" encounters and a handful more, Nikki and I noticed the systemic problems of the divorce industry weren't confined to the legal side. Every step seemed designed to be as acrimonious as possible, and there were people profiting from every barrier they could construct to alternative resolutions. No one we'd seen was interested in listening to our specific concerns and desires, and even if we'd kept searching and found a few who were, they still would have had vested interests in making things combative and making us dependent on them.

Nikki and I have never been too proud or egotistical to seek out good advice and help. We're happy to—we both know we aren't experts in everything. We'd ended up trusting ourselves to guide our own divorce, but the outcome of the legal process was easy to ascertain—either the work was done and filed or it wasn't, and either we'd answered our question, "What's best for Asher?", or we hadn't. Even so, we lined up the right professionals to turn to if we ran into issues in the very beginning.

The next step was to build our post-divorce family, which we wanted to be very different from anything we'd ever seen, but the path forward wasn't clear. As little information as there had been on collaborative divorce, there was absolutely none for this, and now we were running on hopes and good intentions rather than quantifiable goals. It's not like Asher had a meter in the back where we could check his not-fucked-uppedness levels, and we knew every decision could have ramifications that might take years to show up. We'd have been relieved to reach out for guidance, but there far fewer post-divorce professionals than divorce therapists and we couldn't trust what we'd already seen of the field.

At the same time, to me, therapy is like being in a classroom; it's a safe place to pick up theories, but no substitute for what can be learned in the field. Throughout our lives, the best advice and guidance Nikki and I had gotten has rarely come from therapists. We both grew up in strong families with explicit values and ways of doing things. Above all, the importance of family itself had been impressed upon us since we were born. We were also both lucky to grow up in families that ran businesses based on their values, and we learned about the amazing things you can do if you have vision and a good foundation. Building something tangible, like companies, with my family members and with Nikki's has made me appreciate the practical value of the lessons we'd been absorbing and gave me a different insight into our collaborative family goals.

# Nikki

When I'm working to solve a problem or I'm feeling uncomfortable in my own skin, I need to have a project. As my marriage with Ben was ending, I'd started a huge one—a jewelry line called Nicole Khristine—with a close friend who lived in L.A. I poured a lot of time and love into every detail. I enjoyed it and learned a lot; it was gratifying that the jewelry was well-received, but it hadn't helped me solve the problems I had been facing.

After the divorce was finalized, I started to reflect more on the woman and mother I wanted to be, and everything was on the table for review. When I took a hard look at my motivations and interests, I had to admit that it was a bad time to be wrapped up in a business venture on the opposite coast—both personally and economically. Closing up shop wasn't easy, but it gave me the time and space to work through other things in my life.

Part of the draw of starting the business when I did had been to get away from the house and away from Ben. Before we'd decided to get divorced, we'd been like ships in the night; sharing a home like that can feel lonelier than being alone. Now that we had faced the scariest part, signed all the legal documents, and were working hard at building our new post-divorce family, I didn't need to find reasons to be away anymore. At the same time, with Nicole Khristine, I'd released something creative of my own into the world, which had been nerve-wracking and exhilarating. I had moved to San Francisco when I was nineteen to work for the 49ers, and I've worked for the DeBartolo Foundation since I moved to Tampa. I've always enjoyed working for my family, but it was exciting to work on something that just reflected me and my interests.

As I was considering leaving my jewelry business, it was hard for me to deal with my conflicted feelings about being a stay-at-home mom. It didn't make sense; I had always dreamed of being a mother, and it was (and is) the best thing in my life. Watching my own mom dedicate her life to her marriage and her children, I had known since I was very young that it was absolutely what I'd wanted. Everyone laughs about how my dad and I are almost same person, how we argue and exist in the world in very similar ways, but I had always wanted my mom's job: I wanted a family to take care of.

In the area and the community my mother grew up in, if it was economically feasible for a woman to get married and focus her attention solely on raising children, that was what was expected of her. Over the past seventy years, women with different aspirations have been fighting to get us every right and opportunity to pursue careers outside the home, and they've won so many hard battles. Unfortunately, rather than expanding the field of respectable choices for women, the messaging now skews the other way—that a woman who chooses to focus exclusively on her children is somehow lacking. It seems like a complicated issue for contemporary moms, no matter what our career statuses are. As uncomfortable as it made me, somewhere along the line, I had subconsciously picked up a fear of not having a career completely separate from my child. I feared being "only" a mom, and believed that motherhood wasn't supposed to be "enough" for me.

Closing down my first public creative endeavor on the heels of my divorce was eye-opening. I didn't have a meltdown. I had branded the jewelry line with my name, but when it was finished—well, I wasn't. The whole experience wasn't happy, but it clarified some things I had been afraid to even let myself question. It helped me understand that I, personally, don't rely on what I'm doing professionally to form the foundation of my identity. I'm an amazing friend, a fiercely loyal daughter and sister, and a creative force to be reckoned with. I'm a masterful planner and social coordinator, and I love helping people everywhere I can. Most importantly—not "only"—I'm an incredible mom. I also don't go easy on myself. I'm proud that I'm still growing. I hope I never stop looking around, taking on new projects, and being unsettled. I realized that "unsettled" doesn't mean "unhappy." It keeps me searching for better, trying new things, and refusing to settle for less than I know is possible.

As I was grappling with the jewelry business and my tough self-examinations, making sure Asher was getting more comfortable and adjusted to the divorce were still my absolute top priorities. He'd expressed some confusion and pain in the beginning, but even that tapered off in less time than we'd expected. Ben and I had decided on a policy of being open and honest with him, while still protecting him from any details or experiences that would hurt far more than help. He heard how we answered him and what we told him, but more than anything, he seemed to watch how we'd acted. As we continued to spend time together as a family and with him individually, he became visibly more comfortable and I was able to watch some of his anxiety dissipate. We worked to assure him he was in no danger of losing us and that he would never have to choose between us. Ben and I were surprised how our crazy experimental family kept getting noticeably smoother and better. Asher adjusted, and that sped up the pace at which Ben and I adjusted.

I realized early on that you cannot separate yourself from your family history. Even though it may not be obvious, your parents' life and relationship affect you for your entire life. My parents have been together for over fifty years. They were high school sweethearts;

Dad was only sixteen years old when he saw Mom for the first time, sitting on the bleachers at a football game. He pointed her out that day to his friend and announced he was going to marry her, and he was right. They got married right after my father finished college. My parents' goals have always included honoring their marriage, but people grow a lot between the ages of sixteen and seventy. As they have changed, their needs, actions, and understanding of what form that honor should take have shifted too.

They raised three daughters together in Youngstown, Ohio, the same place they'd grown up, so they could instill in us the same values they cherished. It was a community of men and women who worked hard for their families, who treated others with respect, who made it home in time for dinner. Being raised there, surrounded by people who took such pride in their families, centered me and taught me what it meant to truly value and cherish my family.

The urge to express my love through food and the hospitality of my kitchen run strongly through my veins; like with my own family today, it is all tied together. Mom showed her incredible devotion to my father, sisters, and me with each and every meal. Growing up, her kitchen was the center of our family life. She made breakfast every morning while we'd sit around the high-top table tucked into the nook where we would always talk before school. My sisters and I would return to the kitchen right after school and perch around the table again for our snacks. We were always in the kitchen because it housed so much more than just food—it was the right spot for family discussions and report card reveals and art projects and quiet time with Mom.

Growing up as a DeBartolo, sharing dinner has always been inextricably tied to my ideas about family. The most important moments of my childhood were not huge, spectacular events—they were our nightly family dinners. Each evening when we sat down, we committed again to our sense of purpose and place within the family and honored our history and our future. Food is the reason the family came to the U.S. in the first place. After my great-grandmother was suddenly widowed, she emigrated from Italy to Youngstown, while seven months pregnant with my grandfather, so that her children didn't starve. She remarried another Italian immigrant, but even with everyone's backbreaking efforts, the whole family still went to bed hungry some nights. Papa respectfully adopted his stepfather's last name, DeBartolo, then he made it famous across the country. But he ate lunch every day at Paonessa's, the restaurant he named after his birth father. He sat at his special small table in the corner and took phone calls while he slowly finished his plate of veal with peppers (his order never varied). He always intertwined family, business, and meal time.

Where Papa's heart truly belonged, though, wasn't in that dark corner at Paonessa's, but around the table at home. Papa worked thirteen to fifteen hours a day, including weekends and holidays, well into his seventies, but nothing was more important to him than being home every night for dinner. His wife, my Nana, cooked for the family three times a day. After Nana died, Papa dined with us three or four nights a week in Youngstown (always in a three-piece suit—I don't think I ever saw him in anything else). For Papa, dinner was always an homage to family, a habit and value he passed down to my father. When I was growing up, even when Dad's business was in San Francisco, he tried to be home every night for dinner. When he couldn't make it home, he tried to bring us with him. Being parents were some of the first roles Mom and Dad had together, and in this early stage of their marriage, they focused on protecting and nurturing my sisters and me. They worked well and hard together. They valued each other and what the other contributed in a way that made me very comfortable as a child, something I wanted to provide to Asher.

As a child, our family dinners always included a large circle of friends. We'd all head to our sides without even thinking—guys sat at one end of the table, and the girls sat at the other. It was very traditionally Italian, incredibly fun, and the memories hold a special place in my heart. Sitting down to dinner with the people we cared about, I learned that we can make our own families—a lesson I eventually turned into a lifestyle. I didn't have the exact recipe yet, but judging from the view around that table, I knew it involved being fiercely loving and committed and loyal, hearty servings of great food, and a lot of playful bickering.

When Ben and I were married, we thrived at giant, boisterous family dinners, but we didn't balance each other out when it was just the two of us. One of the keys to my parents' success has certainly been that my mother is a very tolerant person; she was definitely the one who bent and contorted herself more over the years. In contrast, neither Ben nor I had been willing to bend in our relationship. Neither of us could accept the other for exactly who they were, both good and bad qualities. And neither of us ever showed any real interest in making substantive changes to ourselves or our lives to make it work.

My mother has a theory about the path she believes every marriage takes, which she calls the "Y in the road." Her idea is that when people get married, they're together at the very bottom of the Y, and as they continue on together, they'll come across that split in the middle more quickly than they'd realized. The wife goes to the left, trying to take care of the child, take care of the house, and do all the domestic things, while the husband goes to the right, trying to find himself, because he really doesn't know who he is yet. A lot of things happen in that part of the Y while they're not together, and it's very hard to come back together the further they split apart. A Y doesn't come back together at the top, it simply ends, and if the couple keeps following the split, so will the relationship.

My mother has an incredible balancing effect on my father, and they've always complemented one another—but really, the main reason my parents' marriage has been so successful is that they've always worked at it. My parents had rough times, like all relationships, but they avoided divorce because they've always worked hard to make sure their marriage was just right; when it wasn't anywhere close, they worked even harder to get it back. Mom and Dad had the additional stress of spending the majority of their marriage in the public eye. They faced many difficult situations together; they worked through their issues as they arose. Their marriage philosophy has always been that if something is broken, you don't throw it away—you fix it. Their marriage isn't a great model because they are preternaturally perfect together, living a fairy tale—it's an amazing model because they have diligently and constantly built it, searched for balance, rededicated and recommitted to one another, and put forth great energy.

For all its charm, Youngstown was run by traditional Italian Catholic men with traditional values, particularly about the roles of wives and women. Marriages were hierarchies, and the men were the bosses. The men could do what they wanted to do, and the women had to do what was expected of them. No one asked much or even thought much about what women wanted to do. Even my parents were like that, to a certain extent. I don't think that it would have been problematic for my dad if my mom had wanted a career outside the home, but it had been culturally ingrained in both of them that it just wasn't expected or done. My mother had maintained a "proper" life, wondering in the back of her mind for a long time if that was really what she wanted.

Mom let my father have the limelight while we were growing up; she was happy in the background for many years. She wasn't interested in a career; she had always wanted to get married and have kids. As she told me, "When you're raising kids, if you're doing it right, you can't put yourself first. You can't be the top dog." It's something I definitely learned by example from my mother, and it's a philosophy I have brought to being a mother myself.

As their love story matured, their values changed. My mother struggled through lung cancer and associated awful health issues for quite some time. After she recovered, something shifted inside her, and it's been an incredible transformation. Mom, who had always been in the background, became a social butterfly. I feel like she's become more herself—she's less reserved, she's happier, and she no longer takes shit from anyone.

My father is the same person he's always been, but we've seen a new side of him too, a more flexible, adaptable side than we guessed he had. If you had asked my sisters and me when we were growing up if he would be able to handle sharing the spotlight with my mother, or even to step back to let her have it, we would have laughed. Dad has a huge personality, and he loves the attention his antics usually get him; watching him stand back and support her is watching him find new ways to tell her he loves her. He's really an incredibly thoughtful person, and he promotes her. Still, when my parents walk into Mom's restaurant, Sacred Pepper, Mom is clearly tickled by the fawning staff, while Dad looks a little green with envy. Every once in a while, he gets a little unglued about all of these changes, but he doesn't fight her on any of it.

The shift I saw in their relationship that helped me most in my own evolving life was watching them start spending time apart. Since my mother blossomed into herself, she has wanted to try new things. She and my dad bought a house in Beverly Hills, and she started planning girls' trips to L.A. each summer with my sisters and me. She made new friends and started exploring interests she never knew she had, even when they took her away from my father's side. My father, on the other hand, started spending more time at their ranch in Montana, working on the real estate business from his remote office. My mother will spend a month and a half in L.A. while my father heads happily to Montana. After experiencing how comfortable my parents were spending time together when I was growing up, witnessing how comfortable they were spending time apart, pursuing their own interests, was interesting. Not only were they both happy, their marriage bond seemed even stronger.

How many people can be so lucky, though? How could I count on finding a partner who made me happy while we were together and supported me while we were apart? Seemed like a one in a million shot.

But I had a sneaking suspicion I was already holding the winning numbers. I just needed to dial them and find out.

# Chad

My keys caught against the edge of my phone as I pulled them from my pocket, and my cell tumbled to the ground facedown. I examined the edges carefully—not even a scratch. The screen lit up properly, and it hadn't dialed anyone. Good to go.

I was a microsecond away from putting it back into my pocket when the screen lit up again—incoming call. When I saw who it was, I wondered if I would have been better off if my phone had shattered into a million unusable pieces.

Don't answer it! Think of all the work you've had to do to get past her!

I shook my head. This was the rare battle my voice of reason couldn't win. No matter how much work I did, I would never get over her. What had it been, a year? Not great, but I think I would have answered the phone even if she'd waited twenty. Steeling myself, I picked up the call.

"Hi, how's it going?"

"Hi, Chad."

Just hearing Nikki's voice broke my heart all over again. Maybe next time, don't answer.

"Can we meet?"

"Why, Nikki? What good would that do?" It was a bold, if futile, effort at self-preservation.

"I really need to talk to you."

Absolutely not! "Okay, sure."

My head buzzed as we hammered out the time and place, and by the time we hung up a few minutes later, my voice of reason had packed up his bags and left. I didn't care—in just a few hours, I was going to see her again.

Just to be clear, I'm not that guy. I don't go into tailspins about anything, much less anyone. Nikki and I had been friends for close to a decade before I fell in love with her. When it happened, though, I fell hard—and promptly got my heart broken.

I knew Nikki was something special from the moment I met her. Her family reached out to the Sheriff's Office to help coordinate safety measures when they moved to Tampa in 2000, and I was assigned to the detail. The initial security briefing was all in a day's work—until she walked in at the last moment, and time stood still for me. She was incredibly beautiful, of course, but that wasn't all—she was magnetic. Meeting Nikki for the first time was like seeing my best friend after a long separation, like she was someone I'd been missing, someone I already had great memories with. There was something exciting, wonderful, and comfortable between us, and we formed an instant, organic connection.

It wasn't love at first sight. Neither one of us were thinking about riding off into the sunset together or pining away for each other— much less considering that we'd end up together. It felt like there was something bigger than the current situation pulling us together. We shared a premonition that we would be important in each other's lives.

Our initial impressions held true, and we were great friends from the very first day. I was focused on my career, working crazy hours on the S.W.A.T. team, and putting myself through school. Nikki was excited about her upcoming wedding to Ben and nervous about her cross-country move. We were living very different lives, but we always felt in-sync with each other. We never had to force conversation, no matter how much time we spent together—and, as I frequently worked Nikki's security detail, we were together a lot. I enjoyed the whole DeBartolo crew so much that I was happy to lend a hand whenever they needed it, even after I moved into different positions in the police department.

Nikki and I remained close friends, and I got to experience so much alongside her—everything from big events and traveling to more day-to-day life. I knew and loved Asher from the day he was born, and I watched as Ben and Nikki grew apart with sadness because I saw the pain they were both in. My deep care, respect, and admiration for Nikki only grew as I saw how focused she was on Asher throughout the divorce process. When the divorce was finalized, I didn't have to restrain my love for Nikki anymore.

Nikki and I had a conversation about our feelings for each other. She cared for me, but she wasn't willing to confuse Asher; she wouldn't introduce a new man into their life before she was certain he was the one. I understood that, but I'd never felt like this about anyone. I knew dating her casually would drive me crazy. I told her it had to be everything or nothing. She chose nothing. I was crushed, and we stopped speaking.

That conversation had been nearly a year ago, and I hadn't seen her at all in eight or nine months. I rushed to get ready. I didn't care if she broke my heart all over again—I couldn't wait to see her.

We'd agreed to meet in the parking lot of the grocery store exactly halfway between her house and mine at seven. Pulling in, I saw she'd beaten me there—not surprising, because Nikki was always on time or early.

She was still in her car, preoccupied reading something on her phone with the engine still running.

I approached the car and tapped on the passenger's side window.

The smile she gave me as she rolled down the window was complicated, but I'd missed it so much.

"Climb in," she said. "Let's talk for a minute first."

We sat in that idling car for the next two hours and talked through everything. Nikki told me that the time was right and she knew what she wanted. She was ready to make our relationship work.

If I still wanted to be with her, there were just two caveats: I had to love Asher and accept his place in Nikki's life. And I had to accept Ben's place in Asher's life.

I would have sacrificed anything to be with Nikki, and she tells me all I have to do is respect her family? Love Asher, who I already loved like a son? Okay, it would be strange to have Ben so involved in our life together, but it was not a bad tradeoff for getting the thing I wanted most in this world. Obviously, I accepted right away.

Even though the relationship was incredible, it wasn't always easy. Being with Nikki, I changed and grew a lot. For starters, my job had been my life; I'd always defined myself through my work ethic. When I was thirteen, I lied about being fifteen so I could start busing tables for a dollar a day, and I've been hustling ever since. I dug ditches (literally) for sewers during the day and unloaded boxes at UPS at night to put myself through school. Once I found my calling as a police officer, I worked the craziest hours, details, and assignments. Midnights, holidays, Narcotics, Warrants, and Intelligence—I've done and learned everything I could to become the best I could be. I joined the force to give back, to make the agency and the community better, and I always put my job first. I didn't know any different, and I never wanted to know any different—until I fell in love with Nikki.

I'd been waiting my whole life to fall in love, and I didn't even know it. I'd given up on the idea that I could love someone the way I loved Nikki. All of a sudden, I was only happy when I was with her. After a great weekend, getting in the car to go to work seemed torturous. I didn't want to leave her. I wanted to get up and work out with her, get breakfast, take a trip. Being in a relationship with her made me realize how much I'd been missing. Asher and I genuinely loved each other, and I spent as much time with him as I could. They made me want to put family first, and I started trying to improve my work-life balance.

The transition from working for the DeBartolos to being part of the family was also awkward and difficult in the beginning. For years, I had been on the job, and as nice as they had always been to me, I'd stood beside the table, looking outward for trouble. Sitting down to have dinner and interacting with all of them in a new way was strange. Nikki's family could not have been more gracious and welcoming I just needed time to change my own mindset. Luckily, I also grew up with a big, boisterous extended Italian family, so once I got my head on straight, I felt right at home.

I was already friends with Nikki's friends, since we'd been going out and traveling together forever, so that transition was seamless. In fact, the only people who ever gave me a hard time were a few people in my own life. A close friend I'd often worked security with judged me harshly for dating someone I had once guarded. I heard whispers that I was with her for the wrong reasons, but that was sheer jealousy. Anyone who has ever spent time in the same room as us could tell I was crazy about Nikki. I would have lived in a car if I could have lived in it with her.

Nikki made me a better person. We are polar opposites: she is outspoken and free-spirited, and I'm regimented and disciplined; she's a Democrat, and I'm a Republican. Traveling is one of her favorite activities, and I'm committed to my stationary job. Our differences work because we share a strong foundation in the importance we place on family. We bring out the best in each other. Nikki is the most generous person I've ever met; she would do anything for anybody.

She really can't give enough of herself and throws herself into helping everyone around her. She has a huge heart and has made me much more open-minded and generous. Police officers see a lot of the bad in the world, but Nikki sees so much good in people, and looking at the world through her eyes and her example has made me a much better, more well-rounded person. The other side of that passionate nature shows when she perceives that someone has been disrespectful, especially of her family—then, watch out, because Hurricane Nikki is coming. That's where I can step in and call a time out, put things in context, and help her see the bigger picture. Together, we maintain an incredible balance and we help each other grow.

I knew pretty quickly that I wanted to ask Nikki to be my wife. If I wanted to share a life with her, though, if I wanted to join her family, I was going to have to figure out how to share it happily with Ben.

In the beginning, I'd carried some resentment towards Ben stretching back to when he was married to Nikki. Even before I grew to love her, I had cared deeply about her and it had hurt me to see her unhappy. From my perspective, she hadn't seemed to be a priority in Ben's life when they were together. I'd really felt that she deserved better, and once we were together, I wanted to give her that.

It didn't help that sometimes it felt like Ben was calling the shots in my relationship when Nikki and I started dating. We were all together frequently because of Asher, and Nikki was careful to include Ben as an equal, so having to account for his schedule and preferences became part of planning my days. All of the together time was hard on me in the beginning. I wondered if Ben had to be there for everything we did, and I thought I wanted more private family time with Nikki and Asher. I'd thought I'd gotten it when Nikki had explained how they wanted their modern family structure to work, but it took me a bit more time to really catch on.

As I grew and changed, I started to appreciate and admire Ben.

I could look back and see how well he'd handled the divorce, and what a huge impact that had on Asher, Nikki, and even me. When a divorce happens, all the pettiness comes out—but Ben and Nikki hadn't gotten petty. They had let everyone around them know that they were going to work through this together. It was a big deal that Ben was the first one to decide that healing was more important than wounding and that their love for Asher could trump anything bad that had ever happened between him and Nikki. I was the child of a bitter divorce, and my parents still haven't forgiven each other. I'd seen how badly it hurt my mother, and I didn't want that for Nikki. I knew how it has affected my relationship with my father, and I didn't want that for Asher.

When I realized that I wanted to commit to Nikki forever, I knew it meant committing to her family—Asher and Ben. Ben and I couldn't just continue to coexist—we needed to build an actual close, caring relationship. I'd seen the way my presence pained him, and though it had gotten better over time, we were still very isolated from each other. For all that time standing in the same rooms, we hadn't had a real conversation since before the divorce.

I needed to reach out to start healing mistakes and make myself vulnerable, and hope Ben would accept and honestly discuss his own emotions and vulnerabilities. What was I supposed to say, though? "I'm sorry for falling in love and finding the person I want to spend the rest of my life with, the person I enjoyed being with the most?"

Eventually, I realized that I wasn't apologizing for being in love, but for being less of a friend to him than I could and should have been. Being there for Nikki and Asher had been my priority, and it still was, but I hadn't realized that being there for them meant also being there for Ben. I'd picked sides, not understanding that there had been no sides to pick. There was just one team—Team Family—and if I wanted to join, I needed the whole team to invite me. I couldn't change the past, but I could commit to being respectful of Ben as we moved forward. From there, I just needed to listen. If our relationship was going to be built on our past, Ben would probably always dislike me, but if it could be built on the future, on how well I treat Asher, on how much I wanted to strengthen the modern family he and Nikki were building—well, then he had every reason to accept me. There was only one way to find out.

I picked up my phone and dialed Ben's number, wondering how awkward one coffee date could possibly be.

# Ben

*I* glared at my phone when it started ringing—who calls in the middle of the game?

I glared at it harder when I saw who it was. Of course—the one guy I know who doesn't watch football.

I briefly contemplated letting it ring through to voicemail. If it was critically important, Nikki or one of her family members would have called. Still, if Chad was calling, it had to be something related to Nikki or Asher. Sighing and muting the television (in the middle of an amazing play, no less), I answered.

"Hey, Chad, what's up?"

"Hi, Ben," Chad replied, calmly and quietly. Chad's voice was nearly always calm and quiet—one difference among several billion between us. "I'd like to speak with you, and I would prefer it if we could sit down together. Are you free right now?"

Watching my team silently fumble and realizing the game was lost, I shrugged. Might as well. "Okay. I'll meet you at the Starbucks on Bay to Bay Boulevard in a few."

## Showing Up

It was extremely difficult for me when Nikki started dating. The first significant man in her new life was Chad, someone who we had both known for years. Even though I had never been as close with

Chad as Nikki was, I'd considered him a mutual friend. He'd sat around our dinner table and shared meals with us when we were a couple. I couldn't help it—I was hurt and felt disrespected that he was dating Nikki.

Seeing him romantically involved with my ex-wife was a major shift in our dynamic, and it took a while for us both to adjust and find our footing in our new roles. Friends have told me that if they were in my position, they could never get close or be comfortable around their ex-spouses' new partners, and I can understand that. Chad and I got used to being in the same room at events like Asher's baseball and flag football games and family parties, and we never had a confrontation, but we were chilly towards each other. I found it especially disconcerting to see him with my son. I spend a lot of time reminding myself that Nikki was probably going to end up with somebody else, and that I needed to want that, to be happy for her, because it was what's best for Asher. The only thing I could hope was for that person to love my son as much as I do and treat him like I would. I had to admit that Chad checked that box, so I could be grateful to him without liking him.

I managed to hang up the phone, get myself together, and make the quick drive over to the Starbucks without questioning or even thinking twice about why Chad would want to meet with me. I was already at the counter before I started getting nervous.

What if he wants advice on how to "deal" with Nikki?

I wouldn't know what to tell him. My relationship with Nikki was getting better all the time, but that was as parents, not as a couple—not even necessarily as people yet. We worked well together because of our shared focus on Asher.

I grabbed my small black coffee as Chad walked in the door. We nodded to each other in greeting.

"I'll grab a table," I said, gesturing to the patio.

"I'll meet you out there."

Without giving it any thought, I headed straight to the table Nikki and I had sat at to work out our divorce. Maybe subconsciously, I knew that table was where difficult conversations and decisions went smoothly.

If Chad was nervous when he walked out to join me, it didn't show.

"Ben, I'm not here to make excuses. I know you were hurt by the way everything happened, and I wish I would have handled things differently."

Starting with an apology? Maybe it is something about that table.

He was right. He and Nikki hadn't always handled their relationship perfectly. I had grievances about the past and concerns about the future, and Chad gave me the time and the space to air all my thoughts. Once we had both said everything we needed to say to each other, he apologized again and promised to be respectful moving forward. He asked for my forgiveness. Then he asked for my blessing.

"I'm planning on asking Nikki to marry me, and your support would mean the world to me. I would also like to enlist Asher's help for my proposal, with your permission."

"I don't know whether to say 'Congratulations,' or 'My condolences,'" I joked.

I was still angry and hurt, but in that moment, I truly understood how committed Chad was to our family, and how important this conversation was for our future. By inviting me to speak, by facing this awkward situation and putting his own feelings and ego aside, by asking me to accept him as part of our family, he had shown respect and loyalty and deep understanding towards what Nikki and I were building. I wanted Nikki to be happy and in love. I saw firsthand how much Chad loved my son, and how much Asher loved Chad. Although it could be incredibly painful at times, I was grateful and relieved for that.

Putting my own ego aside, I gave Chad my blessing and my permission.

I was preoccupied, wondering what types of growing pains were facing my family as Chad and I got up from the table and walked out the door together. Lost in my own thoughts as we reached our cars, I accepted Chad's handshake on autopilot, then changed my mind.

Dropping his hand and pulling him in for a hug, I said, "Congratulations—she's your problem now."

# Nikki

Asher and Chad were conspiring. I hadn't been able to turn a corner in my house without bumping into them together for days, but whenever I stumbled upon them, their urgent, whispered conversations stopped and the huddle scattered. They were up to something sneaky, and it was pretty obvious I was the target... or the mark...or, at the very least, I was a person of interest.

Maybe they were planning a birthday present, or playing spies, or getting into trouble. Maybe I should have been nervous, or checked to make sure no one had broken a window. At the same time, Asher had made it to the wise old age of six without having ever tried to hide something important from me, and I've trusted Chad implicitly since the moment we met. The two of them had known each other since the day Asher was born, and they share a special bond. By this point, I was so crazy about both of them that knowing how much they loved each other made my heart swell. Even if I was being left out, it was hard for me to look at them together and feel anything but happy. I don't love surprises, but I decided not to dig. I held back and waited for their reveal.

It was worth it.

Chad was grinning like a fool in the background as Asher ushered me over to the couch and asked me to sit down. He was taking this job seriously, even though he looked like he was about to burst at the seams with secrets. He knelt on one knee and presented a small box and a big question: "Mommy, will you marry Chad?"

Few moments in life have been as perfect and beautiful as staring into Asher's sly, shy eyes and realizing how excitedly he was anticipating my response. He wanted to know if I approved—he was already all in.

## The New Balance

Nothing about our blended family has been a mistake or an accident. By the time Chad asked me to marry him, Ben and I had spent three years strengthening our post-divorce family and preparing ourselves for the future, and we'd made a lot of progress. Strong, healthy relationships are balancing acts, and we had never found our perfect balance together while we were married. Realizing early how crucial our post-divorce relationship was going to be for Asher, we'd set out to find our new balance.

Ben and I took a huge step towards finding our balance together by tackling one of the most potentially destabilizing elements we could consider—new romantic partners. Though we never really sat down and mapped out exact "rules of engagement," some guidelines formed organically as we worked through every issue. In the beginning, we had no idea how the logistics would play out between the three of us; introducing additional elements was even scarier.

Ben and I were divorced, but we were both very aware that we would never be unattached again. All our actions affected Asher and our family as a whole, and we recognized that additional romantic relationships could complicate every arrangement and goal we had for our collaborative family. It was a critical issue for us to tackle at the onset, because while neither of us rushed from filing the divorce papers to get remarried, we were both out meeting people and going on dates. Between sharing custody and the way we had prioritized establishing two homes for Asher, Ben and I had the space and freedom to see other people. We were able to protect our son from forming attachments to anyone we were uncertain about introducing, shield him from any possible relationship drama, and limit unnecessary additional confusion in his life.

When we talked about the possibility of serious romantic attachments with others in the future, including the idea of new marriages, Ben and I had very different responses. When we got divorced, Ben was adamant that he would never get married again. I didn't discount the possibility for myself, provided the person and the situation were exactly right.

Some divorced people purposefully avoid romantic relationships, or they postpone getting involved with anyone until their children have grown up. I'm sure there are many reasons, but it's common to hear they're trying to avoid confusing their children. With what I already knew about myself at the time of the divorce and what I would learn and accept about myself over the next year, I knew that wasn't the healthiest example I could model for Asher. My own ideas of romance grew and changed with me and with my family. I didn't just need to be swept off my feet—he (whoever "he" was) would have to sweep all of us off our feet. If I met the most amazing man in the world, but he didn't love my son like his own or questioned my close relationship with my ex-husband, I wouldn't have remotely considered bringing him into our lives.

As Ben and I worked to establish our modern family after the divorce, I was frightened to realize that I already had a connection with someone that was much deeper than I'd let myself acknowledge. Chad had been one of the first people I'd met when we moved to Tampa. He'd provided me security—first professionally, then as a friend and confidante. We had a ton of fun together and he could always make me laugh, no matter what situations we were facing. His sensitivity and ability to intuit what people need are incredible gifts, and they help make him a fantastic police officer. Whenever my world was in crisis, he offered steady support, and over the years, our bond had grown incredibly strong. When Chad and I finally had a serious talk about our mutual feelings for each other, though, the certainty he'd expressed in his love for me had been overwhelming. It forced me to make a tough decision.

As deeply as I cared for Chad, Asher's security and happiness were much more important to me. I never wanted Asher to feel like he was competing for my love and attention. Of course, I knew Asher would always be the center of my world, no matter how many things changed or who or what else came into the picture, but he deserved an adjustment period of his own, time to explore how he fit in this brand-new family model. My focus was on minimizing my son's pain and confusion and making our family arrangement stable and viable; there just wasn't enough left over for a serious romantic relationship. I couldn't fully commit to Chad while staying true to my commitment to Asher and Ben, so I distanced myself from him and the situation entirely for a long time.

I needed space to get my head on straight and reprioritize and work on everything in my life. I wanted to come away from the divorce as a better mother and a better person, and to do that, I knew I needed to grow as a person. For the next year, I spent time with Asher and my family, worked on my business, and had a ton of fun with my friends. I went on a few dates and met some great people, but I didn't get seriously involved with anyone. I liked everything about the independence of being single and learning what it meant to be alone. I built a great life for myself very quickly, and my family was pleasantly shocked with how happy I was.

Taking time for myself was a brand-new experience for me. I have never really enjoyed being alone for long periods of time; I'd always been surrounded by family and friends. When I was little, I was such a common fixture in my parents' room at bedtime that they eventually moved a couch in for me. My sisters both left for college when I was twelve, and I felt a little like an only child, which I'd countered by basically moving all of my friends into my home. I love being around people and taking care of people. With the exception of my morning "me time," I love surrounding myself with the energy and love of the people I am close to.

It was fun meeting new people and casually chatting, but over the course of that year, I grew to realize I wanted something more. I appreciate companionship, I like being in a relationship with someone special, and I draw strength from loving and being loved. I love love, and I'd come to recognize this wasn't unhealthy or immature—it was a core part of me. I could be strong and independent and still enjoy taking care of someone and having them take care of me in return. I didn't need to be alone to be a strong woman, to grow, or to be a good mother. Denying myself a relationship that would help me continue to grow as a person wouldn't just be a sacrifice, it would be setting a poor example for my son and offering him a less complete version of everything I could be.

Asher was doing well and my relationship with Ben was getting stronger—my family was in a good place. With a year of hard-earned personal growth under my belt, I was ready to face the emotions I'd set aside in order to focus. As terrifying as it was to admit, my heart already belonged to Chad. Our time apart had been important, but I had done the work I needed to do, and now I had the time and space in my life to commit to him.

Going out to dinner and having a few drinks is a big thing for us. We love going to NYC together, zipping around, seeing shows. We often work out together but, for the most part, we just hang out. As long as we're together, we're happy; we love sharing our lives with each other.

I have grown so much since I moved to Tampa in 2000; in some ways, I feel like almost a completely different person. I am calmer now, I am happier—but when Chad is around, I always seem to be an even better version of myself. He balances out my temper, even though we can both get mad at times. He orients me, and we both thrive under each other's love and attention. It's a powerful dynamic, very similar to my parents' marriage. My father and I have similar temperaments—we can both get worked up. My mother is Dad's opposite, she balances him out, and Chad, who is such a level-headed, even-keeled person, anchors me in the same way. With Chad in my life, I found myself able to breathe deeper and focus harder on the things that make Asher and me happy.

Still, when Chad and I had started talking about the possibility of marriage, I'd been nervous. I loved him, but I wasn't a free agent. Was he ready to commit his entire life to the single question I was laser-focused on: What's best for Asher? How were we going to make Asher feel comfortable with this change? How could we guarantee he'd never feel like he was of secondary importance? Chad was wonderful and perfect for me—but could anyone in the world ever be able to love our son as much as Ben and I did?

With his proposal, Chad had found a way to answer all my questions and worries without saying another word. The proof was right here in front of me; enlisting Asher and making sure we had my son's full support also meant that Chad had successfully enlisted Ben. When Chad asked Ben to meet with him before he proposed, he'd proved to both Ben and me beyond a doubt that he got it. He'd taken me seriously and believed me when I told him that Ben was always going to be a major part of my life. Those two men sat together and realized that they both loved this family enough to commit, not only to Asher and to me, but to each other, forever.

This ring was a promise to all of us. I knew I loved Chad—and

I loved who I was with him in my life. I loved how much he loved my son, and I was ready to love him forever. With Asher and Ben's blessings, we had all officially agreed to add another member to our modern family. I could finally answer yes with my whole heart.

Chad had been dreading asking my dad for his blessing the most, but it turned out to be the easiest. Dad had seen how happy I'd become, which made him realize how truly unhappy I'd been before. My mom, who had adored Chad from the minute they'd met, actually gave us the hardest time. She'd seen how much I had grown and what fun I had being single; she wanted me to consider whether I was really ready to give that up forever. It was another awkward conversation I'm glad we had, and once it was over, it was buried. She had more fun than anyone helping us plan our wedding.

Neither of us had been prepared to fall in love, and when we did, there were no roadmaps for how we could smoothly integrate our relationship into my unorthodox modern family. In hindsight, it's clear that Ben and Asher and I made the right choice by accepting Chad into our life. My house is a happy one. My son is so loved, and he's growing up into an incredible man with the guidance of the best father and stepfather I could possibly dream for him.

I'm actually glad we faced each challenge without being fully prepared. There were so many opportunities for Chad to walk away, for me to ascertain whether this was something I wanted forever, for any of us to realize he couldn't commit to the whole crew. It would have been much easier for us to make a clean break than glide effortlessly into the future. At each step, as we decided to keep going, Chad had to consciously recommit to me, Asher, Ben, and our ideas about the family we were determined to build. Likewise, I had to consciously decide, over and over, that Chad was the right fit for my family, and it strengthened my already steel resolve to make my family work. By the time Asher led me up the aisle towards Chad, rocking out to the

Queen song he'd selected for his entrance as ring bearer, I knew we were all going to give it everything we had.

# *Ben*

When I gave Chad and Nikki my blessing, I meant it. I knew Chad was madly, deeply in love with Nikki, and that he would be great for her. He wanted to give her the type of love and the marriage that she and I hadn't been able to build with each other. More importantly, I could see clearly that he loved Asher like his own son. I knew it was important for Asher to have a male role model even when he wasn't at my house, and I wanted the best for him. Chad was everything I could ever hope and ask for in a stepfather, and I knew he would be great for and to Asher. To give Chad and Nikki anything less than my full support would have been purely selfish. I would have been acting from my hurt ego, which would have been wrong and destructive.

I don't claim it was all perfect right away. We didn't all bond overnight and wake up the next day as a cohesive blended family. Loving Chad was hard for me at first, and loving me was hard for Chad. I'd done a lot of work since the divorce process had started to control my ego, but I still had a long way to go. It was tough to watch him with my son, knowing that he was another father when I wasn't there. Even though I knew it was the best thing for Asher, even though I knew Chad wasn't a threat to my relationship with my son, even though I knew Asher loved us both, my pride would swell up and stick in my throat. Chad and I both had to swallow our pride and grit our teeth, and if anyone had taken a good look at either of our faces during a long day out as a family, they probably could have almost seen our lips moving, chanting I've got to be okay, I've got to be okay under our breaths. It worked—we worked diligently on loving each other until what was in our hearts matched what we knew in our heads, and now we're better than okay. Our bond and enjoyment of each other is genuine; we will go to sporting events and UFC tournaments with each other. I feel really lucky to count Chad as a friend. Even on grumpy days, we can take comfort in seeing that the way we get under each other's skin proves that we are, without a doubt, family.

In some ways (including the most important way), the period after the divorce was a good time. I made sure to make the time as good as possible for Asher. I followed my own father's example to show my son that actions speak louder than words. As a father and as a person, when I was on, I was on. I could be charming and wonderful, a really attentive father, but I could also shut down and silo myself off from everyone. I knew I was a committed, loving, and generally good father, but I also knew that I needed to do more—everything—to show Asher how much I loved him and how proud of him I was. Going into my own world had affected my marriage. It hadn't been healthy in my relationship with Nikki, and I knew I couldn't risk it affecting Asher the same way. When I got divorced, I really became a good father on a whole new level. Having Asher for half of the time meant there was no way I could escape inside my own thoughts. It really forced me to step up, and it still does, even today. Splitting custody evenly makes me remember how much I need to prioritize my son and my family every four days. There's no room for slacking, no way to take it for granted.

# Identity Issues

I had a lot to fix in my life after the divorce. Realizing I was accountable for who I was in every way and that I still needed to examine some gaping holes in myself was a tough process. I knew that I was not still wrapped up in Nikki and our marriage, so I thought I was done with all of it, but I had not considered some of the identity issues I was facing. I was in my late thirties, and I had never worked through who I really was—which parts of my identity had been provided for me and which were intrinsic to myself.

From the minute I was born, I'd been recognized as one of the Swigs. In San Francisco, my family had been very well-known and well-respected for generations. The Swigs owned the iconic Fairmont Hotel and supported the arts and were prominent philanthropists. It was an identity, this thing outside of myself that people ascribed to me that I had no control over. Growing up, it felt like something good. I used it as a shield, and it worked—I didn't have to worry about who I was inside, and for a long time, everyone thought that everything in my life was perfect. I learned that if the outsides look good, then everyone assumes the insides are just as good.

When I married Nikki, I switched identities and titles. I became Mr. D's son-in-law. It had been an even bigger, better shield, and it had covered all the imperfections and insecurities and emptiness I'd felt. I hadn't needed to work through my issues for a long time because I thought if no one else could see them, they didn't exist.

Mr. D had come to my hometown at a very strange and dark point in its history. When everyone felt scared and sad, he helped unite us around the San Francisco 49ers as a symbol of hope and healing. When the team won the Super Bowl in 1981, it was the first ever championship for San Francisco, and it gave us something to celebrate. I'm not exaggerating when I say that Mr. D was one of my childhood heroes, a man I had never known but long admired.

When Mr. D owned the San Francisco 49ers, he created one of the best franchises in NFL history. He viewed himself as working together with his players and staff towards their mutual goal—winning the Super Bowl. Mr. D was the owner, but he did more than any owner ever had before—he gave the team everything in his power. He provided them with an incredible coach, key players, restful accommodations, good facilities. But he also knew their kids' names, knew their wives, knew what was important to them because it was important to him. He treated those players like his own kids and friends and family, and the players responded to that. They saw him putting everything he had into his role, and they put everything they had into their own in response. They played as hard as they could out on the field; they watched out for each other; they were a family. None of the players could have performed Mr. D's role, and Mr. D could not have performed theirs, but all together they made something incredibly special.

I'd been interested in exploring all different types of investing, but after Nikki and I started dating, I went to work for Mr. D. I transitioned with the business to Florida after Nikki and I got married, and I stayed with the company for some time after the divorce.

Mr. D is one of the nicest, most genuine people I've ever known. We've stayed very close since the divorce, and we joke about how I'm his favorite ex-son-in-law. (It's an exclusive club—I'm the only one.) He treated me like a son from the day we met, and he still does. The strength of his character and his love has never wavered. During the earliest, most tempestuous days of the divorce, my mother was terrified for me, knowing I would feel very lost and alone for some time. When she reached out to Mr. D, he looked her straight in the eye and assured her that he would always watch over me.

His support and encouragement have always allowed me to learn and try things I wouldn't have been able to do myself. All the way back in 2002, I went into his office and told him I wanted to go back to school to get my MBA; I thought it would help me in the company and in my career. Mr. D raised his eyebrow at me and said, "I'll get you an MBA."

Both Mr. D and his father had graduated from Notre Dame. In a funny twist, his father never applied. He'd planned to continue working for his stepfather's company after high school, but his mother wasn't happy about it. At the last minute, Mr. D's father hitched a ride with his cousin to campus and talked his way in. He had to pour concrete for construction crews from eleven at night to seven each morning to pay his way through, but he'd still managed to earn a degree in civil engineering in four years. The DeBartolo family generously supports the school, thanking them for taking a chance that helped shape their collective success.

Both Mr. D and I laughed as he picked up the phone and pretended he was dialing the dean.

When he hung up the receiver, he told me, "Look, you don't need an MBA. You just shadow me. I will copy you on every email, invite you to every meeting, and you'll learn the most you ever could." He had been running incredible and diverse businesses for decades; he'd learned from his father, a gifted and driven businessman. He'd also taken the time and implemented his talents to find alternative paths and diversify the company considerably. I knew he had more business acumen than the entire faculty of any business school, and this was a once-in-a-lifetime offer.

Sure enough, I was able to sit in and take notes for every business meeting, and I mean all of them—local, traveling around the country, family meetings, executive meetings, and so on. He also put every resource he had at my disposal so that afterwards I could knock on office doors and ask for explanations of anything I hadn't understood. (I really racked up some hours in the doorway of the accounting office.) He was right—I came away from that experience with more operational skills than I could have ever dreamed.

Learning under his tutelage was a privilege I will never be able to repay or forget. I saw the way he operated and ran businesses all over the world, from sporting interests to development and investments. His teaching methods weren't formal and he never lectured—we just did things together and we talked. Along with all the applicable knowledge, I gained some things I could have never learned in a classroom. I learned to confidently identify my talents and became comfortable using them. He taught me to turn ideals into action and how valuable my ability to absorb information is, to trust myself and my instincts in business and in life. He was a true mentor; he showed me how to put every ounce of heart, character, and business acumen into every decision, and then he gave me the space to grow on my own in the directions I needed to.

As I examined my life after the divorce, though, I realized I needed to make changes in my career. I was Executive Vice-President of Diversified Holdings. I was on track to be very successful, but I was miserable. I wasn't doing anything except focusing on my career, and it didn't play to my strengths. I have a flair for the forty-thousand-foot view, the opposite of the detailed work I was doing. I couldn't keep working at a job that made it harder for me to be emotionally available to my son. He deserved more from me in the moment, and he deserved a better example for the future.

I felt like I was in the position I was in because of who I was related to, not because of what I was capable of doing. If I was ever going to figure out who I was and what I could accomplish, I knew I needed to get rid of this crutch. Even so, I was addicted to the visibility I had as part of Mr. D's orbit of influence, and I was scared to give it up. It would take an incredible friend and an amazing opportunity to make me take the leap.

Within a month of meeting Nikki, I also met the best friend I've ever made, my brother-by-choice and business partner-for-life, Farhad. We instantly bonded and quickly realized how well we worked together. Farhad had been throwing raves since college, and I decided to invest in one. On our very first project together, we got Mix Master Mike to be the headliner. The Beastie Boys are my absolute favorite group (I think I'm the lost member), so it was a pretty auspicious start to our business. We became best friends very quickly.

After Nikki and I got married, Farhad approached me with an interesting real estate transaction in Oakland. It was called Murder Alley—it was run-down, in a bad area, and impossible to finance, but the numbers looked right. We needed a million dollars in cash to buy it outright. Neither one of us had that type of money lying around in a spare suitcase, so I'd worked up the nerve and went to Mr. D. Without question, he'd written us a check.

Don't get me wrong—people looked over it and did their due diligence. There was a meeting where the family had to approve it, and I had been working for DeBartolo Holdings long enough for him to know my integrity—this didn't fall out of anyone's back pocket. But Mr. D absolutely didn't have to do that; no one, myself included, would have ever faulted him for passing. His generosity is legendary.

Farhad and I took our obligations regarding the loan very seriously. Mr. D never put any pressure on us; he wasn't counting the days until he got back the money. In fact, we paid him back shortly after our first sale, and I walked the check up to his office myself. He was surprised. He looked at it, laughed, looked at me, and said, "I didn't think I would see a penny of this back." It was a proud day for me, and an important start in a slow shift in my identity. Mr. D had lent his son-in-law a million dollars—but he was paid back by a legitimate businessman.

That loan launched our business. Farhad and I are 50/50 partners, and we've grown our holdings slowly and methodically from there.

We fixed up that piece of property, flipped it, and then did the same for a second property in Alameda. Over the years, our real estate company has turned into something pretty big, which is exciting—but that doesn't even begin to describe the impact it's had on our lives.

Farhad and I share values and vision. We both have so many other things we value in life besides work, especially our children. We became fathers for the first time at nearly the same moment. Asher is three months older than his son Kingston, so they've known each other their whole lives. We've been able to raise our kids together, even across the country. We've leaned on each other through the years for fatherhood advice. Whenever I bring the family to San Francisco, we all go over to my mom's house so the kids can hang out and bond. Farhad even calls my mother "Nana Patty." Neither of us is reckless, and we expand the business thoughtfully, so we don't have to spend all our time on the job. We talk nearly every day, and I've always valued his insight because he is not, and never has been, a yes-man. We have a genuine, loving friendship—the rarest type.

I know I can count on Farhad for anything. If I called him and told him there was an emergency, that I needed money, or that he needed to be on a plane and be here immediately, I know he would absolutely do it. No questions. We're incredibly truthful with each other, and we trust each other's judgment; we both know neither of us would ask for any type of sacrifice if it wasn't a real crisis. My life is better because I know that he's one of the people I can always turn to.

The moment came when I decided it was time to turn to Farhad, and to our business, and to invest all my working time and energy into that. It was a huge leap of faith, and it wasn't always easy. When I left DeBartolo Holdings, my ego was huge yet fragile, and my identity was still set in my unofficial titles. Without all of that, who was I? Detoxing from the DeBartolo orbit and building an identity that didn't rely on a surname shield took some time and a lot of work, but it all helped me build the most incredible career I could imagine.

These days, I joke about being a serial entrepreneur, I focus on early-stage investing. I'm a natural starter, an idea guy. Usually I start a company, find an operating partner, help get it moving, then step back and watch it come into its own. Once one of my businesses is established, I'm always there to help and advise, but I spend most of my time looking at it from the forty-thousand-foot view, my prime location.

Even as I was transitioning out of the business, Mr. D assured me that he would always take care of me. He still provides back office services through DeBartolo Holdings for my businesses today—tax, legal, and accounting help. It's a huge expense and burden I don't have to deal with, and it means everything. I know I can always go to him for help or advice if I need it, and I still go to the office in Tampa every now and then. Mr. D spends a lot of his time these days in Montana, working from his office on his ranch, but we see each other pretty frequently at holidays and dinners and get-togethers.

I love what I do professionally, but it's not the most important thing to me. My job is never number one. It can be chaotic and messy and risky, but it employs all my best skills and gives me the freedom I need to take care of what's really important to me. My family is number one, my life's work, and the kids are the most important part. It took some time, but in the process of growing and reflecting after my divorce, I figured out that the American Dream, for me, was to control my own destiny, be able to come and go as I want, take summers off, and travel around the country with my family in Cletus (my RV and part of the family).

# Ben

I am a creature of habit. If someone wanted to murder me, I would be the easiest target in the world because my routine very rarely changes. After Nikki and I split up, every Friday night when I didn't have Asher, I would go to a 7:30 meeting, then meet some friends at Ciccio and Tony's for dinner. We always sat at the bar.

One Friday night, we were having our usual dinner when this absolutely gorgeous girl walked in and lit up the room. We all had to stop talking so we could pick our jaws off the floor. There were only two major issues. One, she walked in with another guy, so I assumed they were together, and two, I had no shot with her.

Their table wasn't ready, so they came and sat down on the two empty seats right next to me. The gorgeous girl immediately left for the restroom, but her friend stayed at the bar. An attractive waitress started talking to him, and the conversation I overheard made me question whether he was in a relationship. He was either single or he was the biggest douchebag in the world.

When the gorgeous girl came back to the bar, the waitress immediately scrambled away. Watching the woman flee, the gorgeous girl turned to her friend and spoke some beautiful words: "Did I just cock block you again?"

THEY WEREN'T A COUPLE. THEY WEREN'T A COUPLE!

It is funny, because I probably come across as having a big ego (and I guess I do), but when it comes to women, I am not the kind of guy who can easily walk up and start talking. I always needed an excuse or an opening, like a mutual friend, to make the first move and get me over that fear of rejection. So, I began talking with her friend, whose name, I discovered, was Jason.

Eventually, the gorgeous girl joined the conversation, and I learned her name as well: Nadia. She turned out to be not only the most exotic woman I have ever seen, but also one of the smartest. I remember thinking to myself, She isn't human—she is a unicorn. It was too good to be true.

They never ended up going to their table. They stayed at the bar with us and had their dinner.

After Ciccio's, my friends and I always went down the street to a bar called The Green Lemon. I invited Jason to join us (when all I cared about was getting Nadia there—sorry, Jason). I held the door as we walked out of Ciccio's and put my hand on Nadia's lower back to guide her through. I felt an energy from that touch that I had never felt before. (Later, Nadia revealed to me that she'd felt the same energy.) After some time at The Green Lemon, Nadia and Jason were ready to head out for the night. I asked Nadia if I could take her out, and she said yes and gave me her number.

There is some unwritten dating rule that says you are supposed to wait a few days to call a woman after you meet. I tried, I really tried—until one the next afternoon, when I broke down and called her. She said she was making chili and invited me over. I immediately said yes. It was the best chili I have ever had.

I drove home that night thinking to myself that I was in big trouble. I knew that Nadia wasn't going to be a fling or casual relationship, but I was still in the middle of a divorce and dead set on living the bachelor life.

When I got divorced, I swore I'd never get remarried. I never wanted Asher to be negatively affected by my relationships, and I couldn't conceive of a woman who would be able to fit into our blended family dynamic. Even after Chad stepped in to become a fantastic stepfather, I was stubbornly insistent—if anything, the fact that Nikki had found someone I could begrudgingly see was perfect for what we were building meant there was even less of a chance that I'd ever meet anyone who fit the bill. That was just lightning striking twice.

When my parents' marriage ended, my father was starting a new business; he threw himself into that and into making a home for my siblings and me. He bought the house he'd always wanted, ten blocks away from my mother's home, and hired a decorator to make everyone's room the same as our childhood bedrooms. For him, it was a period of reengaging with us. He had custody every Wednesday and every other weekend. After the divorce, he was very committed, and he was more present for us than he'd ever been.

When my dad remarried, it definitely changed things. Diane, his new wife, was a very domineering stepmother. She was very focused on impressions and having the perfect family, and I truly believe that step kids weren't a part of that image. She wanted to be a mother, so when she came into my dad's life and saw my siblings and me, she decided to try to mother us. Not only were her ideas about what it meant to be a mother very strange and divisive (she would always choose favorites and try to play us off each other for gifts and things), but even if she'd chosen better tactics, there was no vacancy in the department. We already had a mom, an incredible one.

My father tried to integrate us all into a family with his new marriage, but it was awful. None of my siblings were fans of Diane, but she and I clashed the worst. We were oil and water. One year, I showed up for the Christmas card photograph with my hair bleached white, and she lost it. She wouldn't let my siblings and me sit in certain rooms of the house, and Nick and I ended up being basically sequestered in the basement. After Diane had her own children, our half-brother Will and half-sister Dede, my siblings and I were pretty thoroughly dismissed. She caused a lot of hurt in our family and created distance between my father and me that took a long time to fix. I wasn't ever going to let someone like her come between my son and me.

Nadia is an incredible person though, just so beautiful inside and out, and I fell in love with her immediately. She wasn't pushing for anything, but I started wooing her right away as though our spark was the real thing—and it was. I desperately wanted to be with her, but I also desperately did not. There were a lot of factors working against us. I was recently divorced; I didn't want Asher to have an evil stepmother; and I didn't even think it was possible that I could be happy in another marriage. I was still working through so many of the issues I had identified when I considered my part in the end of my first marriage, and I was focused on having a good time and being the best father to Asher. No factor was working harder against me than myself. I was in love with Nadia, I wanted to have her in my life, but I still wanted to be out doing whatever I wanted to do. I wanted the best of both worlds—to have my cake and eat it, too. In short, I was an asshole.

I really was the worst boyfriend, although it took me a while to even earn that title. Every time Nadia would demand to know if we were together, I would be squirrely about it: "I'm being as good as I can be." "I'm doing the best I can." When Nadia finally called me out and told me she was going to start seeing other people too, I couldn't handle it. I broke and agreed that we were in a committed relationship. Even then, I was lying. I didn't want Nadia to move on, but I was determined to do whatever I wanted to do. All in all, I cheated on her for two years.

# Becoming Who I Wanted to Be

When I met Nadia, I had changed, but not enough. It wasn't a question with a deep answer, but Nadia still had to help me find it: I was a jerk. I was who I was acting like, and I was acting horribly towards her. At a certain point, enough was enough, and she was done with my shit. She moved out, got a new place, got a new car, and moved on with her life. For five weeks, I thought I was fine with that—and then suddenly, I realized I absolutely wasn't. I showed up on her doorstep, crying and begging her to come back. We finally had a real conversation, and she made me see that I wasn't taking accountability for myself.

My behavior, for years, had been awful. Somewhere inside myself, I knew I needed to change, but I wasn't ready and I didn't want to. I was pretending that I was this good guy who happened to slip up sometimes, and that just wasn't true. I would take accountability for specific little moments and incidents, but I refused to acknowledge that, in the big picture, I wasn't a good guy at all. It was something Nadia had been trying to make me understand for quite a while. When she'd told people, like her mother, about the things I'd done to her, I'd been outraged: "You can't tell people! You can't tell your mother! She'll hate me!" Nadia's response was to force me to take responsibility for my actions, to make me understand it wasn't her job to prop up my good-guy fantasy. If I didn't want people to hate me, it was on me to not give them a reason to hate me. If I didn't want to be a jerk, I had to stop being one, not just excuse all my actions as mistakes.

I finally got it, and I took accountability: Yes, I'd been unfaithful to her, all over town, every step of the way, behind her back. I heard myself clearly for the first time, and I realized I needed to make some more major changes. The work I had been doing on myself after my divorce wasn't enough; I had learned to take accountability for the part I'd played in my divorce, but I hadn't applied any of it to how I needed to act in relationships afterwards. When I am in enough pain, when I know I need to make a change, I know I need to turn to a higher power, and I am willing to do anything to find more tools to help me get through and get better. I participated in the Landmark Forum, a personal development seminar that focuses on accepting accountability and understanding your part. I don't know that I learned any additional tools from Landmark that I hadn't known from the twelve steps, but they were both teaching the same things about being honest and true with yourself, and it helped me to hear it again and take the time to dig deep within. I learned a lot about myself, and I came to the realization that through all of the breakups and reunions, my life was better with Nadia in it than without. To keep her, I needed to be a better person.

## My Grounding Measure

Building trust with Nadia took time, and it happened in layers, but she saw my participation in the Landmark seminars as a sign that she hadn't hallucinated the part of me that she loved. It was enough for her to stick around, and it ended up being a turning point for us as a couple.

Our relationship isn't perfect and it never will be, but we work on everything. We never tried to bury our inauspicious history. It's important to us to be honest with ourselves and each other so we can never forget how much we had to struggle to get where we are today. We can even joke now that Nadia has been with me for nine years and I've been with her for seven. I get away with a lot, but there are absolute limits. She doesn't sweat every little thing, but she's also not flexible at all when it comes to her lines in the sand. If I ever betray her again, I know she would be completely finished with me. It took years and prodigious effort on her part to learn to trust me, and I know she'd never be willing to do that again. There are things I do and don't do to preserve our love, and I know I'm responsible and accountable to make sure I never hurt her that way again.

Nadia is the perfect combination of sweet, unspoiled, and smart. Even at twenty-six, when I first met her, she had unique wisdom and a sense of humor that helped me find perspective. She was so far from any stereotype. She treated everyone with respect and kindness, and she was genuinely interested in what people had to say and what they were experiencing. She was younger and smoking hot, but she wasn't shallow; her beauty radiated from how aware she was of the world around her. She wasn't materialistic, and she wasn't worried about impressing anyone. She likes beautiful things, but she doesn't get a huge shopping high. Most people will make compromises for money or influence; Nadia has the natural strength of character to stay true to herself while enjoying creature comforts that other people would kill for. She could walk away from it all unfazed and still be exactly who she is. The things that make her happiest in life are her kids, her dogs, and me, which helped me detox from leaving my central place in my family and the orbit around the DeBartolo family. As a couple, we have more space and time to get to be our own people. We can enjoy family vacations and dinners and the company of everyone we love, and we don't have to be in the center of it all. We very much have our own private nest going on, even while still being fully engaged in our larger blended family.

I travel a lot for work, and sometimes I just need to get away, which Nadia's fine with, even with two very small children at home. Just recently, she bought me a bell that I keep upstairs in my room so I don't have to yell down for coffee. I know I can be, on the surface, completely ridiculous, and everyone knows Nadia is a saint, but we have very compatible personalities and needs. There's no power struggle between us; we both know who we are. We accept each other and share a deep mutual respect. If something does bother her, she tells me and we fix it, clear the air, and move on. I know she's not going to hide her pain or silently suffer in a situation where she's miserable. Nadia can communicate with me in ways that break through, even when I get lost in my own head, and we share a lot with each other. She's absolutely a confidante, which is very new for me. I never had just one person I felt I could trust with everything.

I joke that I'm going to have a Howard Hughes room in our new house so I have a good spot to descend into madness, but Nadia pulls me out of my hole a lot. I've needed to adjust to the new energy balance in our home since Izzy and Jackson have joined us, and Nadia understands that sometimes I need to retreat and do seven things at once, and she's great about keeping everyone away while I decompress. At the same time, I know that when the family invades, it's time to welcome them. They'll venture into my mancave for visits, and it's a good space to spend time together. I was a lot more social when I got divorced, just trying to keep myself busy, but I can go a long time now without hanging out with anyone outside my family. I participate in family life more than I ever have, and I know that I can't check out completely anymore, but I don't always like being around people. Nadia understands and empathizes with that, and she doesn't ask me to participate in everything. She might not even tell me when she's having family or friends over, because I can choose if I want to be involved or not. I know that she'll draw the line and let me know if I actually do need to come downstairs or interact with someone. When she tells me I need to be there for something, I know it's important because she doesn't make me come to every last thing.

When we met, Nadia was a party person. I've always been very upfront about my sobriety; it's important to me, and it's not going to change for any relationship, so it was one of the first things I told her about myself. She was intrigued; she'd wanted to get sober for some time, and she liked being with someone who had done it and wasn't a bore. Three or four months after we met, I threw her a birthday party, and she decided afterwards that she was ready to stop drinking. She's never had another drink. Sharing sobriety as a common value is incredible and means so much to me—it's another layer, a spiritual connection, that I'm so happy to share with the woman I love.

She is very confident and sure of herself, and it projects clearly in how she thinks and talks. She let me know from the beginning that she was committed to finishing her master's, getting married, and having babies. I didn't want to get remarried or have more kids, so I tried to talk her out of it every step of the way. She was very clear that she wasn't interested in bullying me into anything. While she was still in school, she was fine being in a relationship that wasn't going to lead to marriage, but it had an expiration date. She was ready to walk away from it all. She wasn't going to give up on her plans and dreams, and it was up to me to decide whether I was in.

Our dating life was a wreck a lot of the time. She seemed to move out every few months because of something stupid I did. I would plead with her for a couple of weeks until she came back, without ever really changing my actions or my mind about what I wanted. The last time we fought and she left, I could sense that this was it, my very last chance. I finally realized that my life was better with her in it, but not without a little help.

I'd been worried when I first introduced Nadia to my modern family; I'd had no idea how Nikki was going to respond. I don't like to play "what if," but if either Nikki or I had ever tried to introduce people into our family who didn't love Asher, who saw him more as an inconvenience than as our incredible son, our happy divorce probably wouldn't have ended up this way. It was the one element in the background that we always knew could derail everything we were building. Even though I was positive Nadia loved Asher like her own already, I was nervous to see if Nikki agreed. From day one, though, Nikki gracefully and organically accepted Nadia into Asher's life, my life, and our family life. There was never any tension or weirdness about it; they liked each other, and they allowed their relationship grow slowly and naturally. I say it's like a twelve-step program, where everyone there can bond over having been in hell—Nikki and Nadia had the shared experience of being with me.

During that last breakup, Nikki was the one who told me, in no uncertain terms, that I was an idiot, that Nadia was great, and that I was screwing everything up. Then she threw the bombshell: "Do you want to end up alone and miserable?" She knew that would hit home. All of this time, I'd been so anxious to avoid giving Asher an evil stepmother that I hadn't considered how shutting myself off from a healthy, loving relationship, how committing to being lonely and dysfunctional, was essentially growing the same results all by myself. That was the moment I realized I had to face my fears and really commit.

Nadia believed that good relationships required constant work, that it was easy to fall into traps and bad habits, and that families needed to be honest and keep the lines of communication open without nagging. She wasn't willing to settle for less than a family that committed to each other, loved one another, and worked through things. She wanted everyone to work on being a whole, happy person while doing everything they could to make sure all the other members were whole and happy too. She loved kids so much, and she had loved Asher with all her heart since the first time they'd met. When I asked myself *What's best for Asher?*, I had to admit it—she was perfect for my son, me, and my blended family. Everything about her aligned with our philosophy and how we wanted our family to work. She wouldn't just be a great fit: She would make us all better and stronger.

It wasn't the first time Nikki had saved my butt in this relationship. Both Nikki and my mother had gotten on the phone with Nadia and worked to convince her that the man who seemed chronically unable to be loyal to her just wasn't me. It was hard for Nikki to believe how awful I was being; I had been a great boyfriend to her, even if I ended up being a pretty lousy husband. Nadia had gotten a really terrible boyfriend, the absolute worst, but I was suddenly sure I could give her a fantastic husband.

Nadia and I got back together, but now I knew the clock was ticking. I had a short window to make things right, or I knew I'd lose her forever. Within three months, I was on the phone with Nikki again, building up my courage. She was the last person I spoke with before I proposed.

Nadia was in shock. She loved me and she was happy—but she had no logical reason to believe I was a changed man. I was asking her to take a crazy gamble, and I knew I'd have to work hard to make her feel safe and loved. She wouldn't end up being completely convinced I wanted to marry her until a year after our wedding, but she didn't even consider keeping me on ice. She said yes.

# Nadia

On the night that I met Ben, he proudly flashed me a picture of his almost three-year-old son. I thought it was sweet that this guy was a proud papa, but I had never dated anyone with children before for two simple reasons—one, I didn't want to fall in love with someone else's child, and two, I didn't want to deal with any baby mamas.

Ben was quickly shoved into the "most likely a problem" category. Still, I couldn't help but feel an overwhelming attraction to his chisel jaw and big brown eyes, and this bizarre ease I felt in his presence. Despite the red flag, I was absolutely excited and wondering if he would call.

Ben called me the very next day, which I found confident and impressive. He came to my house and we walked my three dogs. I remember he boldly grabbed my hand, and at that moment I thought, *This guy is either going to be the greatest thing in my life or the worst thing that ever happened to me.*

That night, I asked Ben about his son's mother. He said she was his best friend, but things between them had not worked out. I respected that. My roommate at the time, Jason, was my best friend. We had also dated, long before, but we'd realized we were meant to be friends instead. Ben spoke highly of his ex. He even told me that she and I would get along very well. Mental eye roll. I did not believe him.

Nor did I believe that he owned a record label. I started to get the feeling that this tall, dark, and handsome man was too good to be true.

When I asked his marital status, he stammered, "Well, I'm…I'm going through a divorce."

I laughed and said, "You're not divorced yet, though?"

"I'm separated," he said.

"I'm sorry, you seem really nice, but I've learned my lesson the hard way with this. I'm not getting involved with someone who isn't divorced yet, and certainly not with someone who has a child. I would never interfere with that."

I had been through one terrible relationship after another; I wouldn't say I was bitter, but I was absolutely running out of faith in men. In many ways, I'd been derailed from life in general. I've always been on the grind, one way or the other, sometimes good, sometimes bad. From my early teen years, I'd struggled with addiction and crippling anxiety; I'd dropped out of college at twenty and suffered grave losses. Prior to meeting Ben, though, I'd finally found some direction in my life. At twenty-six, I'd refueled my passion to become a therapist. I was back in college with the goal of attending graduate school and becoming a licensed clinical social worker so that eventually I could work in private practice. I knew I wanted children, and I'd decided to get my life in order so that by my mid-thirties I could have them—with or without a husband (not super realistic in retrospect, but the truth). Very little was going to deter me from this path.

I decided to put Ben in the "friends with benefits" category, which he was on-board with. Ben was not interested in a commitment, as he was just coming out of a marriage. I wasn't interested in committing to a guy who needed to sow his oats and who wasn't sure if he wanted to get married again. We dated, though, and Ben did adorable things, like sending me an entire skeleton so that I could study for my anatomy class. He introduced me to his mother the very next time she came to Tampa. He even threw me a birthday party.

Complete sobriety was necessary to accomplish my goals and dreams in life. When I met Ben, I was on track but I still struggled with alcohol. Meeting Ben gave me that final piece to my puzzle. I had never met a sober person I could relate to, who I could admire. (Now, because of Ben, I know so many.) Ben was my first sober friend…and certainly my first sober boyfriend! It's hard to explain the bond that people in recovery share. Sometimes being sober is like being on an island, because the rest of the world uses alcohol to celebrate, to relax, to communicate and engage, and to commiserate, but we do not. We are very clear and do not have the same buffer. So, while Ben and I were the minority in today's society, we had each other and were not unique within our own community.

Ben sent a lot of mixed messages as well, though. He wanted his freedom and wanted to be on the Tampa single scene, but he tried to make me believe he was devoted to me through his generous actions. I was very focused on school, so his silly games did not bother me. I was not going to be played with. I really liked him, but he had too many issues for me to get too hung up on him. I had already learned in life that if a man didn't say he was committed, I should assume he was playing around with other women.

Eventually, Ben became jealous because I was also dating other people. He told me that he wanted to start being exclusive.

"Yeah…but you don't want to get married or have kids," I said.

"I would have kids, or one kid…maybe, maybe. I just can't think of that right now."

Ben would find great ways to tap dance around the fact that we ultimately wanted different things. Still, I agreed to be exclusive. Ben's integrity regarding his son, his ex-wife, his sobriety, and work had made an impression on me.

Ben wasn't going to introduce me or anyone else to Asher until he knew the relationship was going to work out. I wasn't going to push; I didn't want to get attached to Asher if Ben and I were going to break up.

Ben eventually brought Asher to a BBQ at my friend's house, but we played it like we were all friends. Asher was absolutely adorable, and I could feel my heart melt. About a year after Ben and I started dating, we decided it was time for a proper introduction. Ben and I set up a scenario where I "bumped into" him and Asher at a taco restaurant. We ate tacos and played Uno, and I was astounded at how brilliant he was. I could tell Asher had his reservations about this new female friend of Daddy's, but when he held my hand to cross the street, I was toast. A total goner.

As Asher and I got to know each other, we had so many things in common that we would joke that we shared a brain. Despite my love for him, I made sure to be mindful of Nikki. There was that twisted little part of me that wished she was a piece of shit so that I could scoop up this little baby and make him my own, but I was fully aware that wasn't the case. I knew she was a good mother, and I was careful not to step on her toes. I had complete empathy for this woman who had to turn her young child over each week to her ex and some-young-chick.

I wanted to let Nikki know that I was friendly and not trying to play mommy to her son. On Valentine's Day, Asher and I even made her Valentine cookies.

## Brilliant Little Asher

Asher looked up at me with his big brown eyes. "Do you know my mommy?"

"No, I haven't met your mommy yet." I cast around, looking for a way to quickly change the subject. "Are you done with the blue marker?

Trade ya." I offered up the green one I was holding. He looked like he had more questions but accepted my answer and made the trade. Phew.

This wasn't the first or the last time I had been on the receiving end of this mommy interrogation. Asher was only four, but he was very clever and extremely inquisitive. As we built our relationship—playing games, building forts, and eating tacos—Asher blew me away with his brilliant, intuitive little brain. Once I became part of his daily reality, he wasted no time trying to put the pieces of the puzzle together. Most of his questions (and there were so many) I had answers for, but this one always had me fumbling.

"Are you friends with my mommy?" he would ask.

Sometimes I would chuckle, "No, buddy."

"Why not?"

"Ummmmm…because I don't really know her yet," I would say, hoping his questions would end. I was running out of answers.

Every evening, Asher would have a phone call with his mommy. I could hear him answer her questions about his day and his dinner and what we were doing at that very moment. I often wondered what this woman thought about me being there with her baby. I myself couldn't wait to have children, but I was careful not to "play house" with another woman's child.

One night I was cleaning up the kitchen after dinner when Nikki called for Asher. He passed by me as his conversation was wrapping up and said, "Okay, goodnight, Mommy. I love you more." Then, in one smooth motion, he shoved the phone in my face and said, "Here, talk to my mommy."

I wanted the earth to swallow me whole, but (flushed cheeks and all) I took the phone and said, "Heeeelllo?"

Nikki and I laughed nervously and exchanged awkward hellos for the very first time. We both noted that Asher had told us a lot about each other.

Asher casually walked away while we had our conversation, but that little stinker knew exactly what he'd done! Years later, when Nikki and I began spending more time together, Asher was proud to take credit for making us friends. It still amazes me that in his young little mind, he figured out that this needed to happen. After Asher forced our phone introduction, I would see Nikki at Asher's soccer and football games. When I first met her, I was intimidated and unsure of her, but we always got along very well. She was much more like me than I had anticipated, and as time went on, we embraced each other more and more.

That May, Asher graduated from pre-kindergarten, and Ben invited me to go to the ceremony. I was shocked and terrified and excited. Nikki's entire family was there, and they took up two whole rows. We sat with them, and I was introduced to this giant family. Everyone sized me up but welcomed me warmly. Of course, Nikki's father joked, "What are you doing with this guy?" That is still his joke to this day.

At first, various people would try to stir the pot and tell me stories that painted Nikki in a bad light. It was very easy for me to shut this down, though, because Nikki always treated me kindly and Ben never spoke ill of her. I also knew that Nikki was Asher's mother, and I would not betray that bond. I always felt that if people judged me based on my actions in my early twenties, they probably would have some horrible things to say about me as well.

Nikki became a sort of sounding board for me. She understood Ben like no other, and she could empathize, which was nice, because Ben was a horrible boyfriend. He would be out in the evenings and taking boys' trips while I stayed home and studied and watched Asher. He was, once again, sending very convoluted messages about our future, but I was committed to school, to total sobriety, to it all. I was going to finish my master's. I was going to have a private practice. I was going to have babies. The clock was ticking on Ben in my mind.

If he didn't pull his head out of his ass by the time I graduated, I was absolutely moving on.

Eventually the truth came out: Ben had not been faithful to me, on-and-off, for roughly a year and a half. It was devastating and, to some degree, shocking for me—shocking because I had given him every out (but, at the same time, not shocking, because I found men to be generally disappointing). At this point we did break up, but not for long. Ben would show up at my house, crying, trying to explain that his behavior had been outside of his character. Nikki and Ben's own mother both called me to explain that Ben was NOT this guy. Ben even called my mother to apologize for disrespecting me and to take responsibility for his actions. Through all of the tears and phone calls, though, the most important thing on my mind was Asher—how much I missed him and how this would affect him. Should I try one more time because of this little man involved?

A combination of factors led me back to Ben. I believed him when he said he was in love with me. Despite what my loved ones believed, I believed in him. Well, I believed in him enough to give him another chance.

I was born to be a therapist. I have a deeply compassionate and empathetic heart and an extremely analytical mind. I have a gift; I am able to quickly put things into perspective in relevance to their weight or importance in the grand scheme of life. As time went by, I used this superpower to accept some of Ben's less-desirable behaviors. I knew that his divorce had screwed with his head and his ego. His entire identity was stripped from him when he left his marriage, and it was going to take some time for him to figure out who he was outside of the DeBartolo family and to find his own way.

As much as I tried to understand him and give him a long leash, though, he continued abusing my love and my patience. I was disgusted with him and his ability to take advantage of me when I gave so much and tried so hard. He was treating me like a nanny at times, and I was being stupid. One thing that I am not is a fool—so I left again.

This time, I was done. In the past when we would break up, he would eventually beg, and I would take him back; this time, I was moving on. This time, Ben was fine with me leaving because he didn't want to get married again and (in my opinion) didn't want to grow up.

That lasted about two weeks, and then he wanted to see me. I think he was shocked when I got a new apartment and a new car. He was used to getting whatever he wanted in life. He'd gotten away with so much, and I think he thought he was going to get away with stringing me along until he found a better option. Nikki had called him and told him he was screwing up, that he was being a fool and would end up alone and miserable in life. Ben started showing up, trying to be "friends," even though I insisted he wasn't a friend. He even came by once when my mother was there; he was so obviously miserable that she felt badly for him.

"Nadia, he looks terrible."

"I don't care, Mom. He does the same shit over and over and over."

Ben had a lot of strong women backing him, including my mom, his mom, and his ex-wife. I was shut down and cold, but he kept trying to get yet another chance. I told him that he was all talk, and that he needed to really work on himself as a human being—that all of his twelve-step jargon was a comfortable mask for the fact that he was full of shit and insecurities.

Ben agreed and signed himself up for a Landmark seminar. He started really working on himself. (This was one of the things that made me fall in love with him—his ability to grow, to change, to work on himself.) Finally, I started to see the Benjamin that I loved underneath all of the bullshit; he wasn't just a figment of my imagination. Not too long after we got back together, he proposed. Without hesitation, I said yes. I knew that when Ben finally popped the question, he meant it.

I graduated, and we were married. We now have two more beautiful children. Ben is a far better husband than he ever was a boyfriend! I know that sounds crazy, but it is the absolute truth. He settled down tremendously. He is the man that I have always known he was deep down inside. Ben has come into his own as an individual and discovered new passions outside of his previous identity. We have created a beautiful life together.

After the birth of our first baby, Izzy, my bond with Nikki seemed to grow stronger. I can vividly remember watching her hold Izzy in the hospital when she was born…the love she had in her eyes while she looked at our baby girl made me melt. I knew then they would have a special bond.

We started doing more together, essentially because the kids wanted to be around each other more. Asher couldn't wait to have siblings and to his younger siblings, he was and is a rock star or like Elmo or something. Izzy and Jackson call him Bubba.

Nikki and I eventually went from being co-parents to real friends. Nikki and I call each other "wife" because it's the closest possible term we can find. We are raising a family together. As stay-at-home moms, we are deeply involved with our children and their schedules and our family, so we talk multiple times a day. While we are very similar in many ways (our sense of humor, our nurturing nature, our girl dudeness, or our cursing ability), we are also very different. We were raised in completely different worlds. We have some differing parenting styles, but essentially the same goals—to raise healthy, happy humans who aren't assholes. Nikki is extremely organized and focused, and I am all over the place. She is at times more intense, while I am fairly laid back; she is a homebody like me, but she actually enjoys going out and being social. I rarely do.

Co-parenting with Nikki is surprisingly smooth. I feel like both of us always keep the sanctity of our modern family in the back of our minds. There are times when I am hesitant to tell Nikki something that I think will agitate her. At these times, I remind myself that we love each other and I must trust in the strength of our commitment to each other and our family. As mothers, she and I share a bond and understanding. As friends, we are able to communicate with trust and love. My younger children refer to her and Chad as their stepparents. When I think of their teenage years, I think of how invaluable it will be to have the extra support of Chad and Nikki with the with younger children.

We enjoy family vacations, morning coffee, family dinners. While I think we always put the children's best interest first, with that comes a fierce loyalty and commitment to our modern family. I know this isn't always the case in divorces. In so many ways, it appears that we hit the jackpot with one another. However, every action that led to our modern family was intentional. All four of us committed to doing what was best and most healthy for the big brown-eyed little boy and, later, for all three children. I do believe that having respect and sensitivity for one another helped forge the road toward a manageable relationship. I learned that relinquishing your ego and putting your children first is also what lays the groundwork for a smoother road and a happy divorce.

# Nikki

**W**alking up to the airplane with Chad, holding onto Nadia's wedding dress like it was my own, I realized how far our blended family had already come.

Our second weddings were huge opportunities to bring us closer together, and both Ben and I had made the most of it based on where we were in the healing process. Ben's generous blessing had meant the world to me for my wedding, but we had still both been too raw from the divorce for him to be involved that day. We had been in a very different place, and I wanted the story that day to be about my wedding, not my divorce. By the time Nadia and Ben were married, though, Chad and I were tasked with precious cargo. During Ben's toast to Nadia at the reception, he thanked Chad and me for creating a perfect modern family. (He prefaced it by acknowledging it was possibly the first time in the history of wedding speeches that the ex-wife and her new husband were recognized.) It was a high-water mark at the time, showing us how much closer our blended family had become. We've grown, both in number and emotionally, by leaps and bounds since.

Ben and I were older and wiser. We'd found the right people to spend the rest of our lives with, and we'd learned enough about ourselves and our needs and our weaknesses while we were married to each other for these relationships to work better. We'd gone through a hundred iterations of, "Are we going to be together or not?" with our new loves. Everyone made very conscious choices to become a family, and our bumpy roads back to the altar had helped us construct the tools we would need in the years ahead. We went into our new marriages knowing that the most challenging work was the lifelong commitment, not the ceremony. We were committing to people who would inevitably be great spouses, wonderful stepparents, and the best family members, but there wasn't any space for slack. We all needed to put the work in.

Chad and I share a very simple philosophy when it comes to our relationship: We can't be together if we are apart. No matter what else is going on in our lives, we make time to be together. It's our shared definition of what love looks like. Chad works all hours and is often called away for events and emergencies; I love to travel, both personally and for my work with the family foundation—so arranging all the logistics can be a challenge. The fact that we both see it as an important issue means we both prioritize it, though. When Chad isn't at work, he's with us, his family. He doesn't have other distractions. We put each other first.

For the first year of our marriage, Chad and I weren't apart for a single night. It was hard to keep it up, but we did it as long as we could—sometimes flying and driving all over the place at the strangest hours. At a certain point, we had to recognize the reality of our situation. Things would come up, and it wouldn't always be possible for us to be together every single day.

We knew that our commitment to each other couldn't be some type of vise. The first time we were apart for a night was when my mom had cancer. I went with her to the Cleveland Clinic, and Chad couldn't go. It was a scary time, but on so many levels it has led to amazing discoveries in my family—and helped Chad and me work through one for ourselves. Stressful and awful things, like my mother's cancer, would happen and keep us apart throughout our lives, but good things would happen too. Chad had the opportunity to do elite police training at FBI Headquarters in Quantico, and I enjoy going on trips with my friends and spending time in L.A. with my sisters and mother each summer. We knew we didn't want our desire to spend time together to ever feel like a burden, sacrifice, or hindrance. On the other hand, both Chad and I had experiences in previous relationships with spending so much time away from our partners that we couldn't connect again when we were back together. There was a lot of middle ground between shipwrecked alone on separate deserted islands and chained together at the waist. We just needed to find a good balance for us.

In the end, we set a rule for ourselves. Even when we are apart for an extended period, we cannot go more than two weeks without seeing each other. (We usually can't make it a week and a half without breaking down and figuring out how to get together, and even when we're apart, we still talk several times a day.) This rule has given us the space to make sure we can do what we need and want to do, while prioritizing and honoring our commitment to each other. We are acutely aware that we have to be together and want to be together in order to stay together forever.

Once Ben and Nadia were married, after all the initial dust had settled, I could breathe a little easier. Our modern family hadn't lost our place or changed our minds with this newest shift—everything was still aimed at our goal. We'd added two people who loved us and made us happier and better, who loved our son as much as we did, and who were eager to help us build the family we wanted.

How had we both found new spouses who were so respectful, willing to engage in this experiment, and able to thrive in the group? We have no idea! Relationships are always hard, even when there are only two people to contend with—imagine adding in two more.

It wasn't always easy for Chad and Nadia to understand every detail and decision at first, but they never questioned the plan. We made it clear that Asher was our priority, and since they loved him too, they helped make it work. Once we decided to throw our backs into it and do it, it kept getting better and easier. We all wanted the most incredible life for him, and one of the pleasant side effects was that we couldn't get there without creating happy lives and a vibrant family for all of us.

# Dad 1 and Dad 2

In the earliest days, when Chad, Ben, and I had been the trio of adults in the family, much of the time spent together was tough; we had to slog through an adjustment period and figure out how to work as a team. Simply put, it would have been much easier for Ben if Chad hadn't been there, and much easier for Chad if Ben hadn't been there. They are both wonderful men and fathers, but they are very different people, and the added stress of the situation didn't help matters. Before they'd really started to accept that they were both in this for life, neither would have minded if they'd incidentally and cordially run the other off. We were all fully committed to Asher, but our adult emotions were messy. We couldn't quite comprehend the new roles everyone would have, and they struggled to figure out who was in charge.

It took practice and time to understand with our hearts what we already knew in our heads: No one was dominant, no one was "in charge." Acknowledging our feelings, airing them out, and framing things in terms of What's best for Asher? and the family at large has been an essential component in making everything work. To be part of loving, wholesome relationships, we all had to engage with each other as a family. Ben and Chad are caring and committed, and

The family
enjoying
Christmas Eve
dinner

*2014*

Chad, Asher, and
Ben at Daytona 500

*2014*

Nikki and Izzy
trick-or-treating

*2014*

Izzy and Chad enjoying
dinner with friends

*2014*

Nadia, Nikki, Asher,
and Ben at Nikki
and Chad's 5-year
anniversary party

*2014*

The family at the
Florida State Fair

*2015*

Chad and Asher getting ready
for the Epsy Awards

*2015*

Nadia, Izzy, and Nikki
on a girls' trip

*2015*

Ben, Asher, and
Izzy celebrating
Chad's 47th
birthday

*2015*

Nikki, Asher, Chad, and Ben
at the DeBartolo Family
Foundation Gala

*2015*

Celebrating Nikki
and Chad's 5-year
anniversary

*2015*

Chad, Ben, Asher,
and Nikki off to a
football game

*2016*

Chad, Asher, Ben, and Uncle Don Miggs on a family trip to the Cayman Islands

*2016*

Nikki, Asher, and Ben at a Tampa Bay Lightning hockey game

*2016*

Chad, Nikki, Nadia, and Ben celebrating a friend's wedding

*2017*

Nikki, Ben, Chad, and Nadia celebrating the Fouth of July in Kalispell, Montana

*2017*

The whole family celebrating the Fourth of July

*2017*

Family Christmas photoshoot

*2017*

The family
posing
for more
Christmas
pictures

*2017*

Nikki, Asher,
and Ben posing
for a Christmas
photo

*2017*

Family
portrait

*2018*

Nikki, Asher, and
Ben posing for a
family portrait

*2018*

Nadia
and Nikki
celebrating
Chad's 50th
birthday in
the Bahamas

*2018*

Nadia, Izzy, and
Nikki off to see
Taylor Swift

*2018*

they understood what had to be done—rising above the small hurts and emotions that would inevitably bubble to the surface now and then—so they put their heads down and did it. As we all grew more comfortable, Chad and Ben started growing closer.

Chad, like Ben, came into our family life with personal experience and knowledge of the damage an ugly divorce could do to a child. The animosity that surrounded the end of his parents' marriage had loomed over his entire childhood. His family still hasn't recovered and reconciled, and the decades of bitterness can weigh heavily on them at times. Chad's experiences helped shape his understanding from Asher's perspective. He would have never exposed Asher to a fraction of the pain and confusion he'd felt as a child. It didn't help him view our situation from Ben's angle, but since Ben was far more concerned about Asher than himself, that was something they had in common. Their mutual empathy and concern for Asher was the key to the peace they made.

Ben and Chad are polar opposites, but rather than use that as an excuse to butt heads, they have worked to make their approaches complement each other and give Asher a wider breadth of experience than either could have offered him by themselves. Both of them love spending time with Asher, and by prioritizing group activities with just the three of them, they fostered a genuine mutual respect for each other that has become, over time, a genuine, caring friendship. The three boys go fishing together, they go on trips, they watch sports—even though Chad isn't a sports guy, he would never pass up the opportunity to spend time with the two of them. As incredibly difficult as it can be, Ben has been phenomenally gracious about encouraging Chad and Asher to form another father-and-son relationship apart from his own. Ben doesn't say, "I just have to let it go," but rather, "That's his stepfather, they can have that experience together." He doesn't begrudgingly accept it; he actively encourages it.

Chad was really excited for Ben when Nadia entered the picture, and it was a turning point in Chad and Ben's relationship with each other. Chad thought Nadia was great for Ben, and he was very supportive of them. With Nadia's influence, Ben became more at ease with himself and our family situation; you could almost see him realize we were all going to be okay. There was happiness and relief on Chad's part, because now Ben had found his soulmate, the person he was supposed to be with, his partner. He knew that Ben's happiness was a necessary part of making our family work.

By the time Nadia and Ben got married, Chad and Ben had both dealt with their bruised egos and stopped stepping on each other's toes on purpose, and their relationship has grown so much deeper and richer in the years since. None of us will ever be perfect angels about the whole thing. Unhelpful emotions still come up, and every so often, Chad or Ben will feel a little twinge of jealousy or sadness or anger about something. But those emotions no longer define their interactions. Chad and Ben's relationship will always need constant work—just like the rest of our family, and every other relationship on earth. I'm so proud of them for the time and effort they put into getting where they are, and so grateful that these two amazing men care so deeply for my son. They were willing to do whatever it took to make it through the toughest initial bonding period, and they even turned potential problem areas into strengths.

## The Nadia Specter

When Ben started dating again, I'd catch glimpses on social media or hear details through the grapevine every so often. Ben and I had agreed that he should only bring a new partner around our family if he was sure she was there to stay. I knew that whoever he married was going to be a good person; she was going to be nice to my son;

and she was going to be a great addition to the whole family. The women he was dating all seemed nice enough, but I couldn't see him bringing them home to Mom, so I wasn't worried that he'd introduce them to Asher or me.

The first time I'd heard Nadia's name was from some catty woman at a clothing store, who insisted on telling me about a present Ben had purchased. When I saw her signature on an email sign-up sheet in another store across town soon afterwards, it felt like a sign—all of a sudden, this Nadia character was everywhere! I was more than a little curious by the time Ben picked up his phone.

"So...who is Nadia?"

Even before I met Nadia, I respected the thoughtful and considerate way she was handling the situation. She didn't push to meet Asher, and when they finally did, she showed him the compassion I'd soon recognize as a hallmark of her personality. She realized it was a tricky situation for him, trying to figure everything out and wondering who she was to his dad. She never wanted Asher to be confused, and she never wanted to take my place.

Even though Ben and I were no longer a couple, we were still doing things together as a family all the time. In fact, Chad and Ben and Asher started doing things with each other when I wasn't around very early on. I was out of town for one of the first New Year's Eves after the divorce, and the boys got together to set off fireworks. Asher didn't know anything but being able to have all the adults he loved interact together in the same room, and it must have felt like a mistake that Nadia and I weren't doing that. He had completely orchestrated this solution up all by himself in his little brain. Nadia and I still get a little sniffle-y when we talk about it. In a very real way, Asher was the first one to make sure Nadia was blended into our family.

# Actually Friends

Soon after Asher initiated our first introduction on the phone, Nadia and I saw each other for the first time at one of his soccer games. She and Ben were going to an event right afterwards, so she was dressed beautifully, though a little formally for the field. We didn't really interact that day. She seemed lovely, but she was very young. I wondered if the relationship could last, and how it would affect Asher if she left.

The first time we actually met was at Asher's kindergarten graduation. Ben and I talked it over beforehand, and I told him I would save Nadia a seat if she wanted to come. Asher's cheering squad took up two full rows, and I hadn't considered how intimidating it was going to be with all of the family and friends there before she showed up. (We're not a quiet crew!) In the midst of the happy chaos and noise, she slid into a seat next to me.

My feelings were complicated. I wasn't jealous or conflicted in the slightest about her relationship with Ben, but it was hard to think about another woman stepping in and acting motherly towards my child when I wasn't around. At the same time, I didn't have any desire to hate her, and I certainly didn't want her to be an evil stepmom-type. She was spending time with my son and she had influence in my family, so I wanted her to be incredible. I wanted to know that she was another answer to the "What's best for Asher?" puzzle, but I knew that wants weren't guarantees. I guess I'd been prepared to protect and defend my son and my family if she seemed like the wrong person, because once we'd spent a little time together, I felt a weight lift from my shoulders. She was kind and sweet, and everyone was drawn to her (myself included). She didn't seem to have an agenda or any strange motives; she was funny and insightful and a pleasure to be around. I could tell she genuinely adored Asher and Ben, and I could see her being able to love Asher like her own.

Our friendship has grown over the years. From that first meeting, I knew I needed to be supportive. She was the first (and ultimately ended up being the only) woman that Ben found worthy of introducing, and I welcomed her. If there was any real possibility she would ever join my family, I wanted to start building that relationship with her from the beginning.

I knew it was my job to set the example of how Nadia was going to be treated for all of our friends and family. My loved ones are amazing and generous, and I'm sure they would have been friendly and kind to Nadia without my guidance, but I wanted them to know they didn't need to take "my side."—I wasn't interested in doing sides. I didn't want to hear any gossip about her or comparisons between us, and no one needed to be catty to her to make me feel more secure. We didn't need to be judged against each other, because we weren't in competition. I wasn't interested in having a romantic relationship with Ben and she wasn't trying to replace me in Asher's heart or life. Everyone in my family was very supportive of us and what we wanted to build.

Nadia's deference to my role as Asher's mother was apparent and very comforting from the earliest days. She was always very conscientious about not stepping on my toes, she didn't make unilateral decisions, and she consulted me on my wishes a lot. When Asher stayed with Nadia, she kept me in the loop. I remember being impressed and grateful after certain phone calls: "Asher had a question about this. How would you like me to handle it?" or "He caught me off-guard and I responded like this. I'm so sorry if that is not what I should have done." She never attempted to stage a coup or undermine me.

Nadia is wonderful, but one of the reasons our relationship is so strong is because it was allowed to develop naturally—no one forced it or hurried it. We got very close over time, on our own, as we chose.

Like Chad, she has a calming influence on me. If we are out somewhere and she senses that I'm about to get involved in a situation, she'll make me laugh and calm me down. I know she gets uncomfortable with confrontation, and I care about her feelings so much more than arguing with a stranger. Ben and I have strong personalities, and we both happened to marry incredibly similar, likeable, and supportive people our second time around. We joke that it's good PR for us—if they chose us, we must be okay! Their perspectives and their temperaments have contributed so much to the family we've built.

I know Nadia and I have raised some eyebrows. We've definitely been asked leading questions by people trying to get the "real scoop," like, "Oh, but you're not actually friends, right?" "You're really okay doing your Christmas card together?" Strangers and acquaintances who have never seen us in action seem to think we are making the best of a bad situation, putting brave faces on. They couldn't be more wrong. We probably talk two or three times a day, even when we see each other, and we share everything. Chad teases me that we're already talking when he wakes up, and we're still talking when he goes to bed. Nadia and I are not just situational friends, we're not just very good, or even just best friends—we're family, from the bottom of our hearts.

People still seem surprised that Ben and I can still be so close, so it's almost impossible to explain to them that Nadia and Chad are equally engaged and invested in our plans. Imagine: two (much less four) adults acting…well, like adults! We weren't heartless robots, we just didn't allow ourselves to be controlled by our knee-jerk first emotional reaction. We were each committed to giving Asher as much attention as possible, and Asher could only be in one place at a time, so to maximize the limits of time and space, we had to be together a lot. We decided it sounded better to spend our days with the family than to be routinely trapped with people we were barely tolerating—

so we set out to turn ourselves into that loving family. Why would we choose to be miserable or uncomfortable when we could enjoy, take care of, and support each other?

Nadia and Chad are both secure enough to trust us when Ben comes to visit me in L.A. for a week each summer and stays at my house. They're both three-thousand miles away, but they know our romantic relationship is entirely over and they don't want to interfere with our friendship.

Some people will never believe that we don't secretly loathe each other, but we have also heard from people who are so touched by our relationship that they want guidance in their own. We've had people going through the divorce process tell us how they want to emulate our approach to healing. The way Nadia and I interact is a completely new example, and people start wondering why their standards for how their partners act around their exes aren't different. It is flattering that our friendship could inspire others to think more broadly about what it means to be divorced, what it means to be a stepparent, and what it means to put family first.

## Asher Steals the Spotlight

Asher stole the spotlight for a moment at Ben and Nadia's wedding with a special toast:

> *Hello everybody, I hope you are having a good time. Just wait until you see my dad and me on the dance floor—that's when the real fun will begin!*
>
> *I'm really proud to be my dad's best man: Thank you, Dad!*
>
> *When I started writing this speech, I just said the first words that came to my mind about my dad. "Amazing" was the first one—he's amazing. And he's athletic, a really good dad, he's nice, and he loves music. What more is there to say?*

*Nadia, when I thought of you, I said you were calm and sweet, but could maybe be a little loud in a funny way, and you are always doing schoolwork! I am so glad you are finally done! Congratulations on graduating!*

*When I think of you together, I think about you watching TV, something I really love to do with you both, which is nice.*

*I must also say I feel very lucky that my mom and dad are both able to share this special day together.*

*Dad, I am happy you found someone so nice to love you back and I am so glad to have Nadia as my stepmom.*

*Oh, Dad, good luck, because Nadia told me she wants three more kids—I think she's crazy! I know you and I want two more, and I hope you can make that happen soon.*

*So, everyone, please raise your glasses to Mr. and Mrs. Heldfond. May they have a lifetime of happiness. We love you. Cheers!*

# Nikki

$A$sher had always wanted siblings, so when Ben and Nadia announced that she was pregnant with Izzy, he was thrilled. I was a little worried that he would end up feeling slighted or get lost in the shuffle. Asher's a very adaptable kid, but he'd been an only child his entire life; he'd actually been the only child in the entire extended family on the East Coast for most of that time. Nadia's biggest fear when she was pregnant was worrying about how she was going to be a mother to her biological children and have a stepchild. Eliminating any chance that Asher and his siblings would feel isolated from each other was a major focus for all of us. None of us wanted the kids to call each other half siblings; they don't, and I don't think they'll ever see themselves that way. We have all been very conscientious about including Asher and giving him enough attention, and he has thrived as a big brother. Asher loves those kids, and they adore him. Even as a teenager, he never gets impatient with them—it's quite awe inspiring.

Nadia and I have grown even closer since Izzy was born. We liked each other before, but there was still a certain amount of separation. Holding Izzy in the hospital right after she was born and realizing in tandem with Nadia that I was going to be like a second mother to this little girl was a monumental family-building moment. Izzy's birth erased whatever distance still existed between us, and we started spending a lot of time together. Nadia and Ben welcomed Chad and me in, more than happy to share the love and excitement of their growing family with us. Raising two small children and a teenager is an incredibly different dynamic than when we just had Asher. Ben and Nadia have done such an admirable job making everything with the little kids work and making everything inclusive within the context of our wider unconventional family.

Ben and Nadia know that Chad and I love Izzy and Jackson like they are our own—so much so that they asked us to be their guardians if anything were to ever happen. It is so endlessly rewarding for us to play such a nurturing, significant role in their lives, to all join together to keep building the modern family we wanted.

## Rules, Discipline, and Conflict

Each person who has joined our blended family has given us so much, made us stronger. At the same time, each person has radically changed our dynamic, and there have been some steep learning curves. The conflicts put us in a better position to move forward and we end up rethinking and revising some of our approaches with every addition, but it can be uncomfortable at first. One aspect we addressed extensively with Chad and Nadia when they committed to the family plan was our responsibilities for setting and enforcing the rules for Asher. Chad makes a conscious effort to check his baggage at the door now after work so that he can walk into the house as a dad and a husband and relax, but when he first joined our family, it was tough to always switch gears. Ben actually wasn't bothered much by the Joe Cop approach, but it drove me crazy! Both Ben and I can get very defensive of Asher when someone else challenges or disciplines him, and we'd learned to warn our co-parents before there was an issue.

For years, Ben and I were the final arbiters of what the rules were and what disciplinary action was appropriate for Asher. Nadia and Chad had always been incredibly respectful and supportive of our discipline decisions, even if they disagreed. Ben and I valued their advice and perspectives, but the decisions were ultimately our responsibility. We have different parenting styles (Ben tends to be a little more traditional, while I'm more easygoing), so some of our rules and priorities are different. There are some rules we disagree on but never really argue about (for example, I'll let Asher watch movies that Ben considers a little mature), and ones that we do argue about (Ben is stricter than I am about grades), but we have always tried to keep the core, most important rules the same at both houses.

We didn't fully map out our plans to create a seamless co-parenting experience for all the kids when Izzy and Jackson joined us, and as they got a little older, the dynamic became more complicated. As Ben and Nadia's parenting style as a couple developed, their expectations and disciplinary methods ended up being different than mine in some ways.

By the time Izzy turned two, she was watching Asher like a hawk. Both of his siblings think he's just the coolest, so anything he did, she'd do, and soon enough, anything she did, Jackson would copy. Asher was testing boundaries, and Ben and Nadia became concerned when his younger siblings started emulating some of his behaviors that were too mature for their ages. Frustrated, they decided that trying to run a household with different rules for different children wasn't working.

Ben and Nadia set specific rules for their home, but as a stay-at-home mom, it often fell on Nadia to enforce them. When Nadia started disciplining Asher, their relationship hit a rough patch. It all caused some tension in my relationship with her as well. I wanted to defend Asher, because the rules were changed on him, but I was also irritated that they'd been changed on me. We'd never had an official policy chiseled in stone, but the rules Ben and I established for Asher had always been the last word on the subject. Now it seemed that house rules took supremacy.

For a short period of time, everything got very difficult, but in the end, we all realized there were different parts of the situation we had each been wrong about. Once we all put it in perspective, we could compromise. I realized that this was good practice for Asher—working under different rules, even ones we don't personally prioritize, is a situation every adult faces occasionally. Asher started to understand that he had a lot of control over how his time at Ben and Nadia's house would go. If he continued to break their rules, everything was going to stay bad and get worse. His brother and sister looked up to him and were going to keep imitating him, so he embraced his new role model position.

Nadia recognized that she'd come in with the hammer, and that she needed to change her tactics. She determined that there were certain things she needed to step back from in order to keep the peace—not only with Asher, but with Ben and me as well. She decided she could not set certain expectations without being able to discipline him (that is her parenting philosophy), and she could not discipline him if I did not support it. All that Nadia demands from Asher is that he speaks and behaves respectfully to adults and others within their home and sets a good example for his siblings; other than that, she does not discipline him or play an active role in anything that requires cause and effect (homework, curfew, rules, and so on). Nadia will give her opinion to Ben and me if she thinks something should be addressed or if she is reaching a limit, but she does not establish rules for him.

We all realized that co-parenting between two houses would require having similar rules. We might do things a little differently from house to house, but the standards are the same. None of us are trying to make sure we're the "cooler" parent or make our house more attractive by having looser rules. We get together and talk about the standards, even as Asher gets older and earns more freedom. As Ben realized growing up, if the parents aren't talking, that nothing but an opportunity for a kid to manipulate the situation. We don't leave that type of room for trouble, and Asher has grown up knowing he needs to loop us all in. For example, we've got a constant "Asher's weekend plans" text thread, and Asher lets Ben, Nadia, Chad, and me know what his plans are all in one fell swoop.

## Four Parents

There's some tough stuff, but overall, maintaining our balance as a family seems to get easier in some ways every year. Asher is getting the best between four parents with distinct ideas, values, and expectations. When we started this blended family experiment, he was young, and we were all untested and uncertain. With twelve years now in the rearview mirror, I can confidently say he survived. Asher is the easiest, most respectful, unspoiled, grounded kid I could ever hope for. He's smart and caring and considerate, and he honestly feels lucky to have Nadia and Chad raising him right alongside Ben and me. I might be a little biased, but I think we have gotten the most incredible results that lots of love and work and luck and obsessive planning could produce.

Asher has the most extraordinary capacity for unconditional and unquantifiable love. Experiencing how fiercely and completely he loves all of us as individuals and as a family and recognizing his appreciation for the love we each share are some of the greatest joys of my life. Any seed of jealousy, confusion, or competition that could ever come up between the four of us as parents would whither quickly; there's no doubt he has more than enough love for all of us.

He gets something unique from each of us. He and Ben share an incredible bond. They have so much in common, and whether they are watching sports or playing video games or just talking about their days, their connection is palpable. Nadia pushes him to grow while still acting as a great stabilizing force, and Chad offers perspectives and guidance drawn from an incredibly unique bank of life experiences. I am his home base, the grounding figure and confidante who knows him better and loves him more than even he could ever imagine. I love knowing that when Asher has issues and questions, he has four caring, knowledgeable parents to turn to, each with their own perspectives and strengths. We're able to support each other better too, because while we're all eager to help him and guide him, everyone has blind spots. It's comforting to have three other people we can rely on if one of us doesn't have an answer!

Chad and I place a high value on open communication with Asher, and it's a special priority in our home. Kids have unparalleled access to the world now. Even if we wanted to, we know we couldn't control every dubious path, whether via website, phone, app, or friend, that Asher could stumble across in the next few years. Asher has always told me everything and I trust him, but there's a lot of stuff out there in the world I don't trust. I want to make sure he's always comfortable asking for guidance and help, that he never feels alienated from us or ignored. On school nights, when we sit down for dinner at six, we shut down our phones and internet for the rest of the night (unless we're all doing something together on a device). It helps us wind down, and it's working—Asher has opened up and shared some things that were bothering him. Whether we watch a movie, catch up on a TV show, or play a board game, the three of us spend good evenings together and have every conversation, big or small, that we need to have.

I'm not very worried about Asher's teenage years. He is a great kid who has done well adjusting to whatever life has thrown his way, and he has a sturdy foundation, painstakingly constructed by four parents who would do anything for him. I know the challenges will be different, but we're seasoned blended family vets now, offering quadruple the amount of support and love than any of us could muster alone. It's a pretty crazy competitive advantage!

# Coordination, Communication, and Bonding

Years before we each got remarried, Ben and I recognized that to make our unique family plans work we needed to focus on building three different (though interconnected) types of happiness: our own, each other's, and the collective whole. We needed to take accountability for our own happiness as individuals, but it wasn't going to be enough; we also each had to want the others to be happy, and we had to be happy together as a group. We couldn't be mad, weird, jealous, bitter, or awkward; the happiness of our ex-spouse and our ex-spouse's new partner had to be as important to us as our own.

Ben and I navigated our romantic relationships by trusting that neither of us would bring in anyone who wasn't focused wholeheartedly on Asher's well-being. That requirement was comprehensive, non-negotiable, and complex, but very pure and natural; we never muddied the waters with additional demands, so we found ourselves with people exactly in tune with our goals, plans, and desires. Nadia and Chad are incredible, self-assured, emotionally mature people. They both came into the family with those qualities, and then respectfully honed them to an art form over the years. They didn't replace anything or anyone, and they weren't trying to; they were fantastic, complementary additions. Once it became clear that they were both incredibly committed and loving towards us and our son, we balanced letting the relationships between the four adults grow organically while providing more structure for the group dynamics.

Through some luck and determination, we have all ended up not just loving, but liking each other. Ben and I share friendship based on our life-defining love for our son, Chad and Ben built a respect for each other so strong that they can co-father together, and Nadia and I are best friends and co-conspirators. Even Nadia and Chad are close. They recognized a kindred solidity and kindness in each other right away, and every so often they take the chance to talk one-on-one and share their own concerns and unique perspectives as stepparents.

We've found many ways to work and play together over the years, but without some serious organization, the dinners, vacations, record labels, radio shows, and group outings would never happen. I'm in charge of creating that structure for all of us—constantly communicating with everyone to balance the schedules, staggering travel for Ben and myself, and creating monthly family and co-parenting calendars. Bonding as a family meant doing things together from the beginning, showing Asher we would always be there for him, spending the time to get know each other more fully (even when it was tough), and encouraging a web of special connections to grow between all of us. It didn't start out as constant interaction. We built it up over time, celebrating holidays and special events and occasions as a group whenever we were all in town, regardless of who had custody.

Over time, we realized that sharing our special occasion meals wasn't enough. Special occasions are usually very happy days, but we needed to be able to communicate well every day—happy ones, sad, boring—even the days when everything seems to be on fire. Waiting until there's a fire to have a fire drill is not a good idea, but when we started facing our first real problems as a family, we weren't too proud to admit that having someone to talk to outside ourselves might help. No one was convinced they had all the answers, so we heard each other out and tried new tools to make everything work better. We needed a therapist who could help us articulate concepts to Asher that we didn't have the words for, who encouraged us to try a variety of approaches to forge even stronger bonds. The most important outcome of these meetings were our weekly family dinners. Since there are seven of us living between two households, it's very useful for us to have some alone time to bond together. We uncover new things about each other at each meal, particularly when it comes to the kids.

Our blended family is at our best all together, when our love and patience and interest and passion for each other and this life come out in the most beautiful ways. The group can almost be divided evenly by personalities; my team just got Jackson, but Ben can switch sides at any moment. Izzy and Jackson and I are each high energy in our own ways, and our voices tumble over each other, getting louder and rowdier with every joke and observation. Asher and Chad and Nadia also share an energy, calmer and more settled and grounded. They're more likely to go with the flow; they are very even-keeled. We all joke that Nadia and Asher share a brain; he's been finishing her sentences since he was four. Ben can match my energy any day, even though he might need to escape for a minute into his own world. We give each other complementary energy and characteristics.

As we grew closer, we made the effort to travel together just to have fun experiences with each other, sharing sodas on the beach or hot dogs at sport stadiums. Over time (but faster than we would have ever guessed), those activities stopped being things we knew we had to do—they became things we wanted to do, things that we were excited about and looked forward to. Spending time interacting in different environments teaches us new things about ourselves and each other. Knowing who is shy in crowds, who falls asleep early, and who likes rollercoasters is another way to bolster our internal support system. The closer we get and the more we reveal to each other, the more quickly and effectively we can react when our children are in need. Even if we never put our discovered strengths and weaknesses to good use, the worst-case scenario is that we had fun, shared happier, healthier lives, and confided in each other.

# Ben

There were a lot of moving parts to consider when Nikki and I had our wedding. When I proposed, Nikki had been dreaming of an elaborate fairytale wedding for her entire life; between the black-tie dress code she wanted and the seven-hundred-person guest list our parents insisted on, we quickly realized we weren't going to be able to pull the events off by ourselves. We hired the best wedding planner in the business, and she helped us create a whole Hollywood production of an event. The location, the food, the outfits, and the music were all perfect, and to this day, I've never seen more flowers in one space. The guest list was incredible—my brothers, Nick and Lucas, got to deliver their best man speeches in front of some of their childhood football heroes. It was such a wonderful day that no one wanted it to end, so it stretched into the wee hours of the morning. I don't think any of our guests realized how close we came to having to call the whole thing off.

We'd reserved Grace Cathedral, an Episcopalian church, for our Saturday wedding. Since the DeBartolo family is Catholic and my family is Jewish, we settled on having an Episcopalian minister, a Catholic priest, and a rabbi all officiating. Juggling multiple officials added to the general chaos, and some details slipped through the cracks. When we arrived Friday night at five for our rehearsal, the minister asked us for our marriage certificate, and we all stared blankly at each other—we had forgotten to get it. We didn't need it, right? Wrong. We were told definitively that the church wouldn't allow us to go through with the ceremony without the certificate—even if we promised to get it first thing on Monday. City Hall was closed for the week, and we were just S.O.L.

In a heartbeat, everyone stepped up to work their magic. It was a big group effort—I remember my mom and dad and Mr. D all running around, pulling whatever strings and calling in any favors they could to save the day. Before Nikki and I really even had a chance to let the mess sink in, Willie Brown, the mayor of San Francisco at the time, was on the phone. He personally came down and had a clerk open city hall bright and early on Saturday morning, and we were able to get our certificate and rush off with just enough time to make the wedding.

Weddings are supposed to be happy, and ours definitely was. Sure, I had pre-wedding jitters—doing my hair before the ceremony, I spent a long moment looking myself in the eye and psyching myself up. The idea of spending life with someone, even the right person, felt a lot like getting sober and coming to terms with never having another drink. Nikki and I knew already that we didn't have the easiest of relationships, but we had the most fun together, and over the past three years, I'd proven I could make her laugh hysterically in even the scariest moments. We know now exactly how overwhelmed and underprepared for marriage we were, but even if all of our friends and family had learned to harmonize and told us we were making a mistake, neither of us would have listened—and we're both glad for that. Even though the marriage ended in divorce, I can't say it was a mistake. We each married our best friend that day, and we'd both do everything all over again just to have Asher in our lives.

That's not to say that we didn't make mistakes that day. When Nikki and I fell in love, we were young and dumb. We did not always make the best decisions or take the time to consider the consequences of our actions, and it put enormous strains on our families in several ways. That part in the wedding ceremony where two families are supposed to be joined together? We didn't do that right. Our wedding shouldn't have just been a celebration of our love and commitment as a couple; it should also have intertwined many lives and strengthened our families. Even after everyone jumped in to get the certificate and save the wedding, Nikki and I didn't use our marriage to bond them together. We began making my family feel alienated and isolated early on, and by heavily weighting my relationships with the DeBartolo family, I created a miasma of hurt feelings and painful relationships.

Nikki and I didn't do it intentionally, but we were both aware that we kept hurting our families. During our marriage, as we grew increasingly unhappy as a couple, we couldn't seem to stop. They were swept up by our dysfunction, and we couldn't even prioritize them. Mending these relationships was shoved further and further back, so we could focus on trying to save our marriage. We couldn't even communicate well enough with each other to say, "Hey, we need to fix us," and we were far too scared to try using family issues as a backdoor to our own. We knew how precariously our marriage was balanced, even if we couldn't admit it; acknowledging one thing was wrong could trigger an avalanche, burying us and forcing us to admit that everything was wrong. Thinking of our broader relationships seemed impossible under the stress, and we never understood the full magnitude of how much additional stress we were putting on ourselves and our families by trying to treat our marriage like it didn't touch everyone.

Most of the time, life doesn't present clear and convenient opportunities to take a step back and fix the things we're in the process of breaking. In the course of the day-to-day slog, it takes a lot to acknowledge where we're actively messing up, and Nikki and I never quite got there while we were married. It took the disruption of divorce for us to address our collateral damage. After we took the scariest step, admitting our marriage didn't work, we knew it was time to set right everything we'd started poisoning and everyone we'd wounded.

As we built our modern family, we took the chance to start healing those relationships. The time and energy were right. We had enough momentum going from the ego work we were doing on ourselves to properly view and grow our own relationship, so it made sense to extend that work outwards. Health and happiness do not exist in a vacuum—they are choices, highly influenced by complicated factors like the people around you. Our families were not going to disappear even if we wanted them to (which we didn't!), and as we threw ourselves into our experiment of happy divorce, we needed all the love, acceptance, excitement, and support we could get. We needed to do our parts to make sure that the people around us didn't resent us, to show them we appreciated them (and learn to appreciate them better). We had to invite them to join our new family structure, in ways we maybe hadn't the first time around. Our son loves each and every member of his extended family deeply. Making sure we healed the wounds we had caused wasn't only the right thing to do, it was how we could build the healthiest and happiest world for him.

# Worlds Apart

I'm very close with my family. They are caring, supportive, and kind, objectively some of the coolest people I've ever met. My mother's life revolves around her children—my brothers, sister, and me. (Now that we're all adults, that focus has moved to her twelve grandchildren.) She has given us so much, but teaching us how to truly love and support each other was one of her greatest gifts. When we were young, she gave us every opportunity to practice until we got it perfect, hauling us up to my grandfather's ranch in Sonoma Valley for short weekend trips and long lazy summers. We rarely brought friends along. It was just us, running around, learning how to really enjoy each other's company, and bonding for life. Our family boundaries are more complicated than many. We've always lived and done everything together constantly, and everyone keeps track of everyone else. It can get messy, but it's how we show that we care.

When my parents got divorced, it was hard on my siblings and me, but knowing we had each other meant a lot. We're very protective of each other. My sister is the only girl and the baby, so we especially dote on her. From family arguments to business ideas, to this day, she knows I will always have her back. She was only seven when my parents split up, and she was arguably the one most directly affected by the divorce. My brothers and I did a lot to shield her, but in the process, we buried our own emotions and developed destructive behaviors.

I was crazy about Nikki when we first met, and part of being with Nikki was spending a lot of time with her family. That was fine by me—I was crazy about her family too, and we all hit it off right away. Starting with family dinners, I quickly joined the party, and Nikki and I did everything with them. I love the DeBartolo family; I loved the DeBartolo family before I loved or even met Nikki. Nikki and I were divorced, but she was still my best friend, and I loved her and her family as my own family. Their lifestyle was exciting—we traveled a lot together, and we were all close friends.

I wasn't the only person who felt that way. By the body and blood count, there aren't many members of the DeBartolo family (it's certainly not as big as mine), and they didn't associate much with their extended family. At the core, there's just the original five (as Mr. D still refers to them): Nikki, her father, mother, and two older sisters. They roll deep, though, going everywhere and doing everything with a lot of close friends, whom they consider family. In a way, she was already accustomed to building alternative families and inviting new people into her family. They made their family through bonds of loyalty and friendship and connections. It's one of the reasons why Nikki didn't understand how stepping on my mom's toes was a big deal. We rarely spent time as a couple with my family even before the move to Tampa, but we spent nearly all our time with hers. Spending time with her family was second nature to Nikki. She didn't have another thought about it, and I was having too much fun to think about how my absence was hurting my own family. Nikki wasn't trying to steal me; it was just what she did, and neither of us understood the full ramifications for quite some time.

When my family met Nikki, they could tell we were both very smitten with each other. We were two very young people madly in love. I'm not naturally a touchy feely, lovey dovey person, and my family knows this well, so they could tell my feelings for her were special. I don't think anyone was surprised when we got married, but they were already concerned before we even got engaged about how I seemed to be pulling away from them. My father saw parallels between my relationship with Nikki and some of the portions of his relationship with my mother that caused stress from very early on in their marriage. Like Nikki's family, my mother's parents were very strong influences on Mom and Dad as a young couple, with a lot of say in what everyone was going to do with their time, requirements for activities, to the exclusion of my dad's own parents. He noticed how quickly I had gotten swept up in all of it, like he had as a young man, and how I seemed to be leaving my own family behind. When Mom and Dad were married, they spent all their time with my mom's parents, and never with my dad's mother, who lived in the same county they did. My father became business partners with Mom's father, and I had gone to work for Nikki's dad, so my father had some pretty interesting insights into the whole situation very early on.

From my family's perspective, everything else Nikki and I had done prior to getting married were just warning shots. The first real sign of danger was when I moved to Tampa. I'm still one of the few in my family to ever move away. There are forty or so of us in San Francisco, and a grand total of six who live outside the area. Imagine how everyone reacted when I announced I was moving across the country. My whole family is in the Bay Area, my roots were there, my businesses were established there, and it had better prospects than Tampa. I had committed to work for Mr. D, but it was all very overwhelming for my family. Some of their fears were true. I didn't adjust well to Tampa, and it did put the relationship on an unequal footing very early. I was in DeBartolo territory, thousands of miles from the people who loved me no matter what. I was no longer able to be my own man, I didn't have my support network, and I became increasingly estranged from my family. I was reliant on the DeBartolo family for every need, emotional and financial, and it was not a recipe for good mental health or strong, stable relationships. My family was hurt and felt abandoned, and I handled the whole thing poorly. I made an isolated island out of them, seeing them infrequently for holidays and short visits for years and rarely speaking to them (and when I did, never about my feelings), and when my family would visit us in Florida, everything seemed odd and tense—like they'd just walked into a mystery dinner theater in the second act. The more time Nikki and I spent in Florida, the unhappier I became and the more it seemed to my family like I was losing myself in my relationship.

# Queen Bees

My mother and Nikki don't agree on all of their values and principles, but they share very similar strong personalities. They are both alpha females, queen bees, and natural matriarchs. They're both used to being in charge and getting their own ways, but besides keeping equally spotless houses, it comes out differently in each of them. My mom will drive herself crazy making sure that everything is perfect; the table, for example, always needs to be set properly. (After some trial and error, Nadia even downloaded an app to her phone to remind herself where all the formal silverware goes!) Nikki is much more casual, not fussy or formal at all, but she's a planner and a scheduler, and she doesn't censor her opinions. Neither one of them responds well to other women who need to have control of things, so they butted heads frequently. Their relationship became tempestuous very early, and it didn't get any better as Nikki and I progressed from dating to marriage, relocating to Florida, becoming parents, and getting divorced.

My mother made some mistakes initially. Mom and I have always had a special bond, and she came out very strong when she first met Nikki. My siblings' spouses have all seemed to innately understand the dynamic in my family, respecting my mother's authority and the sacrifices she made over the years for her children, but Nikki was different. She was never outright rude to my mother, but she was still very young and very hotheaded. They clashed frequently (often over things Mom should have blamed me, not Nikki, for), and they got into the habit of putting me in the middle.

The move to Florida put a major strain on all of us, but their relationship grew increasingly problematic after Asher was born. My mother lives for her grandchildren the way that she lived for her children, and Asher was her first. She was so excited during the pregnancy, and she couldn't wait to meet him. She'd naturally planned to come to Florida and be with us after he was born, but as the due date rapidly approached, Nikki got scared. She told me that she didn't want my mom there in the delivery room—she didn't even want her to come to Tampa—and I had to tell her to stay away. Mom wasn't allowed to come down and meet Asher until he was nearly a month old.

In hindsight, both Nikki and I fully agree that we didn't handle this the right way. It still makes me sick to my stomach that I treated my mom that way. I try not to have regrets in life, but that one haunts me. What kind of man does that to his own mother? Nikki knows she should have put her fear aside, and I know I should have stood up for what I knew was right. Instead, we did what we did, and we hurt my mother very deeply.

The gulf between my mother and Nikki, like the one between my family and the DeBartolos, widened over time. Nikki's family is incredibly kind and generous to everyone, but they are extremely close and protective of each other. Our parents and siblings all loved each other, but they weren't one big family. Nikki and I didn't do as much as we should have to make sure everyone was included, so my family would still end up feeling left out of a lot of activities, even when we were all together. My family would come to Montana with us and stay with the DeBartolos on Mr. D's ranch, but looking back at old photos, there was never a picture of all of us together.

## Family is Forever

Even from San Francisco, my family could see the warning signs that my marriage was crumbling. My mother and siblings came to stay with Nikki and me a few times after Asher was born, and they could tell we weren't communicating well. We didn't fight much, but we didn't interact much at all. They could tell I was hurt and that there were things going on. From their perspective, there wasn't really one event that marked the souring of our relationship, but we no longer acted like a young couple in love. They only got glimpses, but I seemed progressively sadder every time they saw me.

When we announced we were getting divorced, some people in my family were angry with Nikki. All of my siblings agree that it's probably pretty tough being married to me, but generally, the feeling was that she had stolen me away and then discarded me. I was living alone without a real support system in Tampa, and to my family, Nikki seemed to have all her family and support around. It took years after my divorce, meeting Nadia, and a lot of work on myself, to start to appreciate the idea that Tampa was home. I know I felt pretty lost, like I was still in a foreign world. My family felt very badly for me. I'd moved to Tampa to be with Nikki and her family, but I was living in a strange place. I was floundering and a little sad, and I had Asher half of the time, so I never had enough time to work everything out for myself. They visited me a lot in the earliest stages of the divorce and transition period, and I was so grateful for their support. I could tell it was painful for all of them to leave me there alone, especially my mother.

I have great relationships and good dialogue with my family, and they are honest and real, but I've never confided in them at the deepest levels. We spoke on the phone often, but I spent years in virtual silence about my marriage. I was absolutely not going to give anyone any information other than that Nikki and I were trying to work things out. I was awful at sharing news with them, much less discussing my feelings, so everything was kind of opaque out in San Francisco. My brothers joke now that it was kind of like I had joined a cult and could no longer communicate with my family. When the divorce became imminent, I finally started opening up to them a little. Despite the years of neglect and my outright self-serving, selfish behavior, when I was getting divorced, they were there to pick me up and love me unconditionally.

I was the most vulnerable the week after the divorce began, and I confided a bit more then, but I was still cognizant of the effects that being completely transparent could have down the road. I think everyone got a little bit of it and everyone had a different role. I would tell my brothers some things, my mother other things, and Farhad different details. By nature, I don't blab; I don't tell stories or use my troubles as weapons to cut down other people, and I wasn't about to start. When I reached out, it was to tap into the strengths of the people I needed, so I would go to them with the pieces that I felt they could help me with the most. I was in pain and sad, but I was also aware that our recent history was not the best representation of us as a couple. Even at my most hurt and angry, I knew it was important to make sure my loved ones didn't feel like it was their jobs to hold a permanent grudge. Somewhere in the back of my mind, I knew that Nikki and I would need all the love and support we could find when we needed to rebuild some semblance of our relationship for Asher's sake.

I'm the only one of my siblings divorced, and ours was the first and only divorce in the DeBartolo family. A parent never wants to see one of their children go through turmoil or something disruptive like a divorce, but our mothers were both particularly worried and anxious for us. None of our parents were thrilled at first, but I don't think they were very surprised. I don't think they thought we were making a huge mistake, though they were sad that we would have to go through something like this.

I know that Mrs. D was really worried about my family when we announced our divorce. Nikki and my mother had been pretty open about the fact that they'd never quite gotten along, but the wider DeBartolo family had always gotten along with my entire family, and still does. Before Nikki and I sat down together for our first coffee date, Mom was trying to protect me. The DeBartolo family was influential in so many areas of my life, and I think one of my mother's worst fears was that they were going to chew me up and spit me out after the divorce. Mrs. D wished there was a way she could reach out and let my family know she and her husband would be there for both Nikki and me while we went through everything, but at the time, she had no idea whether that was going to be possible or true. Those fears have never remotely been realized—they have been incredibly kind to me. Nikki's father has continued to play a big role in my life. The whole DeBartolo family showed me so much sympathy and admiration for how Nikki and I dealt with things from very early on, they never closed ranks around Nikki and they acknowledged everyone's role in what was going on. I knew I needed to examine my relationship with each member of the DeBartolo family and make sure they stood on their own.

There were several different responses from our families when Nikki and I announced the way we wanted to work through our divorce together. Most people were relieved and happy and rooting for us, even if they had no idea how it was going to work. Some people on my side of the family weren't immediately happy. At the same time, everyone was incredibly aware that there was a child involved, and we all wanted to protect him. No one would have done anything to cause Asher any additional hurt, so everyone quickly (though sometimes begrudgingly) respected our decision and offered their support.

# Healing Help

When I committed with Nikki to co-parent Asher and always put his needs first in my life, that was a commitment to my son. I would never have introduced another woman into our lives who would have driven a wedge between us. I couldn't have possibly been with a person who threatened my commitment. In a similar way, I made a commitment to my entire extended family.

After I met Nadia, I wanted her to meet my mother as soon as she could come into town. I realized that part of making sure I didn't replicate the mistakes of my past was prioritizing my own family. I knew I couldn't begin to take this relationship seriously if

Nadia couldn't get along with my mother. I refused to be in another relationship that would get between my mother and me. I'd already been in that situation, and it had fractured my ability to live a complete life. To be a good father to Asher, I needed to be accountable to all of the people I loved. Someone divisive was a deal-breaker. I needed to be with someone who could help me heal the damage I'd already done, and I told Nadia as much before she'd even started meeting my family.

My mom and Nadia loved each other from their first interaction. They are great complements to each other, and they enjoy each other and share a deep respect and mutual admiration—in short, they have a great relationship. My mother is so impressed by Nadia's lack of pretense, and she appreciates the extraordinary values they share. Nadia enjoys talking to my mother, and they share a lot of laughter. She's fascinated by how classy and hippie my mother can be at the same time, and she feels so lucky to be able to consider her family and a friend.

They were also both the right people in the right place to love each other. My mother had learned, through her experiences with Nikki, to temper her approach and listen more carefully to differences in opinion, to appreciate the love of a new family member as the great gift that it is, and to never take it for granted. She freely admits that staying out of her children's lives is not her natural instinct, and it took her a while, but it's something she's learned to do. Nadia's secret weapon, besides being one of the most caring, understanding, unique people I've ever met, is her master's degree in clinical social work and an in-depth background in therapy. Nadia isn't delusional about my family (or anything else). She knows they aren't perfect, and she accepts that they have their own sets of issues and hang-ups like all families, including her own. She brings a different set of tools and a different level of understanding to deal with all these fuzzy emotional situations, and it has made a tremendous difference.

My family was on uncertain footing for a while after my divorce was finalized, still holding a grudge against Nikki and worried about me. Once I started working on myself, got my own place, and met Nadia, my family could see there weren't going to be any nasty lasting scars. Nadia's influence and perspective helped me detox and find myself again very quickly, and my family could tell she was a major contributor to my recovery. She even helped them understand that Nikki wasn't some malicious villain. Whenever something would come up, Nadia reminded everyone that people grow and change quite a bit over a decade. Once my family realized they were still viewing Nikki through actions she'd committed when she was essentially still a child, and that they had the opportunity to have a relationship with the adult, the healing really began.

When Nadia and I got married, it felt like a celebration of us and the love we share for each other, yes, but it was also a celebration of family and togetherness. My second wedding was toned down, much smaller and more intimate than my first. It was a great time—all of my family from San Francisco was there and we all got to spend time together, swimming and playing. Asher was everywhere, and he made a toast. I was older and wiser. From the time that I got married to Nikki to that point, I had changed: My values and priorities had shifted. It was never going to be me and my bride alone. I love Nadia, of course, but we all know I love my children more than anything. Asher shifted my (and Nikki's) dynamic to everything and everyone in our worlds.

## Building the Extended Family We Love

Recognizing how much I had hurt my family and myself by not working on these relationships during my first marriage, I've really prioritized spending more time with them and being more involved in their lives. Reconnecting with my siblings has been incredible, and we've been able to provide so much support for each other. It's cool that, as we get older and everyone faces different challenges in their relationships, I am able to provide some of my hard-earned perspective. Every marriage faces challenges. We like to joke that I paved the way to the new normal. When my brother Nick married into his own mixed family, the groundwork was already set. His wife's ex-husband lives in Germany, but he stays with my mom and comes to all our family holiday events whenever he's in town.

I love learning more about my brother's winery, which he opened on our grandfather's old ranch, and helping my sister take her food blog to the next level. We all have different talents and skills, and it's such a pleasure working with them. My brother Nick has a great network in Silicon Valley, with his finger on the pulse of what's hot out there. Going in on investments with him always feels like an adventure. He's very personable, political, and charismatic, and he gets access to these companies that, with the amount of money we're investing, would usually laugh us out of the room. Lucas has always done work while serving on the board of our family's real estate company. The four of us, along with my mom, are trustees on a family trust. We work together, vetting deals and deciding whether to invest as a group or as individuals. It is like our own little angel group, and it has been so much fun spending time together in that capacity. I am in awe of how smart they all are.

At this point, my family takes a lot of comfort in knowing how close I still am with the DeBartolo family, and how much we all still love each other. From very early in the divorce, my family started to recognize that to be a good father and to be around for Asher, I was going to have to stay in Tampa and carve out my own life—moving away from them was never an option. It was a hard prospect, but everyone saw how much Nikki's family helped the situation, and they were grateful. I'm still all the way across the country from the warm embrace of my San Francisco family, and they are glad I have people here to help take care of me. I'm not married into the DeBartolo family anymore, but everyone recognizes and is incredibly grateful that we're still a family.

Nikki and I have saved our extended families so much strain. We had critically examined our relationships with each other's families, and made sure we could use this redefinition of our interpersonal relationship to create the healthiest bonds with all of our extended families. They see how happy we are, how happy we make each other in our new roles, and how wonderfully Asher is turning out. At this point, our extended families have great rapport, they see each other frequently, and there are no bad feelings left on either side. Everyone is super kind to each other, and they act as though they never stopped being related by marriage. We are all bound together forever, and we'll deal with things like families do.

Even though my marriage to Nikki did not bring our two families together, through hard work and with a lot of support, we made sure our divorce did. I was talking to a friend recently and I realized that in the beginning of the divorce, if you had asked me to write down what I wanted the outcome to be, I would have written that I just wanted to be able to be around Nikki and Asher and not have that palpable tension in the air that makes everyone uncomfortable. I could NEVER have imagined that our relationship and our family would be what it is today.

# Asher

'm a sports fanatic— I like to watch and play almost everything! Dad and Chad and I go on guys' trips together all the time to see football and baseball games, and I've collected some really cool memorabilia and autographs. I'm on my high school golf and lacrosse teams. My core group of best friends are people from school, but I've also met a lot of my friends through sports. Florida is nice because we can run around fields and courts and hang out at the golf course together through the whole winter. It's all really fun… but nothing can beat fishing.

I fish a lot and I'll fish from anywhere—off the docks behind my mom's house or my dad's, around the mangroves, offshore, deep sea, you name it. I even love watching fishing (there are actually a lot of fishing channels). It makes me think about becoming a professional angler when I grow up. I like being on camera, and I'd be pretty great at hosting my own fishing show! I would go around the world on crazy fishing trips, and a camera crew could film me and everything I could catch.

I've been fishing since before I can even remember. I think I was two when I started. Our old house, the one we moved out of when I was three, was on the water too. I remember going out and sitting on the dock, fishing with Mom and Dad when they were still married. I was really young when my parents got divorced, so most of my memories from then are blurry. I only kind of remember when my dad moved out, but I memorized pretty much everything about my dad's new home that he called Boys' Fort. It was wide open, and all the steps were made of glass, and I thought it was cool. I had never lived in a house like that! I couldn't fish from there, but my dad and I played a lot of indoor soccer.

From that point on, I've always had two homes. I don't think of my mom's house or my dad's house as my main one—home is whichever one I'm currently at. Sometimes one house will fit my mood better than the other. I have one house with siblings and one house where I get to be the only child, so I can play with Izzy and Jackson and read them books, but when they're getting too crazy, I can always escape to Mom's house. There are also different rules in both houses. Dad and Nadia's rules are mostly things about the little kids, making sure we don't act in certain ways or say certain things in front of them. Mom and Chad are strict about being clean—Mom is pretty crazy about not getting the house dirty. Whenever I'm going out with my friends, she always makes me give her all the information, but my dad is more easygoing about stuff like that. Sometimes I kind of forget which house I'm at, and I mix up the rules—like oops, I can't do that here! For the most part, though, having different sets of rules means that there's always space for me to do whatever cool things I come up with without making either of my parents crazy. I have a little more independence than most of my friends, because I can do different things at each house, while they usually have to always follow one set of rules.

As cool as it can be to have two homes, there are parts that aren't so great. Shifting from house to house has always been one of the hardest parts of my parents' divorce for me. When it was new and I was really little, moving every week was confusing and it made me a little anxious. Not seeing either my mom or my dad for a whole week was too long, and I would miss whoever I wasn't with too much. My parents were really cool about it, and we all worked together to solve the problem. Even now, I move between the houses every four days instead of every week.

I really don't have a favorite parent—both Mom and Dad are awesome. My dad is as obsessed with sports as I am, so we can talk about those, and he teaches me things about his work. We read a book about how to start your own business last year, and we're still brainstorming about what type of business we'd like to start. On the other hand, I can share anything with my mom—in fact, I'd feel guilty about hiding anything from her. I like to talk to her whenever I have a problem or a question. It's bugged me a few times, like when I need confidential advice and I'm at my dad's, or I need to talk about a great play and I'm at my mom's, that my parents don't live together. It'll hit me, and I'll catch myself getting sad and missing the parent I'm not with.

At the same time, I've never really wished that my parents would have stayed married to each other. Mom and Dad are both really stubborn. They start joke-fights with each other all the time, and they're not even mad, but neither of them can back down! It's funny because they're not being mean to each other, but it's also good for all of us that they can both walk away. I'm also usually happiest when my whole family is together. Without the divorce, I'd never have Chad, Nadia, Izzy and Jackson, and I would have missed out on a lot!

Chad and Nadia are my parents too. They love me like parents, and they argue with me like parents. Now that I'm older, I can go to them for advice or help studying, and they can teach me different things than Mom and Dad. They've both made sure to build relationships with me, not just with each other, since the beginning. Chad has pretty much always been part of my life, and I thought he was so much fun. I remember how happy and excited I was when he asked if he could be my stepdad. Chad had me propose to my mom for him, and I felt very involved in the decision. I don't remember the first time I met Nadia (Dad and I ran into her by accident), but I do remember the second time, at a Mexican restaurant called Chihuahua, when I was five. Dad and Nadia were both nervous that I wouldn't like her, so they made it seem like we had just run into her again to take some of the pressure off. They didn't have to worry—I remember thinking she was great, really funny. She lived with us for a while later on, and we played a lot of animal trivia together. Even though it didn't last long, I remember how bummed I was when Nadia and my dad broke up and she moved out.

I always wanted little brothers and sisters, and I'll never forget the night Dad and Nadia told me I was going to get my wish! I was really excited. We didn't know if it was a boy or girl, but we spent the whole dinner thinking about names. I think everyone was kind of watching me to see how I'd react when I wasn't the only child anymore. When Izzy was born, everything did change. It was crazy, but I wasn't upset about all the attention she was getting. It was actually pretty nice! I was getting older, so I didn't need quite as much care, and having four parents paying all their attention to me all the time was getting intense. Izzy and Jackson are still young, but having a brother and a sister is already everything I wanted it to be.

Sometimes I step back and think about how weird my family is, and I think it's awesome. It's strange to try and picture it any other way, but I know it didn't have to turn out like this at all. A couple of my friends have parents who are divorced, and they seem like they're pretty nice to each other, but they don't spend as much time together as my family does. I'm really glad all four of my parents are best friends. Mom, Dad, Chad, and Nadia have done almost everything together for most of my life, and for all of Izzy and Jackson's lives. The little kids don't even know that what we have together is strange. Izzy told

Dad the other day that she has so many grandparents (more than her friends), and she listed them all. She included Nana (Chad's mom) and Crazy Papa and Kiki, which is what she calls my mom's parents. There was no question in her mind that we are all a family, and she's right. No one could honestly ever tell her any differently.

My family really is great, and because of the work we all put in and the time we all spend with each other, it keeps getting better. My parents have always let me know that they are going to do what is best for me. When they see something they can improve, they'll do whatever they can, big or small. They pay a lot of attention to what's going on, and they also expect me to be honest with them about any problems I have. They knew living in two houses could be tough on me sometimes, so when they saw the chance to get rid of all the bad parts (and keep all the good ones), they took it. When Dad and Nadia announced we were moving right down the block from Mom, I was so happy! The first morning that I woke up in our new house, I walked over and surprised Mom for breakfast. Now I can walk or ride my bike between my two houses, I can fish off whatever dock I want, and I can play with my brother and sister whenever I feel like it. It's like we are all living together, but I still get two houses!

Our Wednesday family dinners are a lot of fun, but my favorite part comes after we clear the table, when I can take Izzy down to the dock with me. I can't wait to really teach my siblings how to fish! Izzy pays attention while I bait the hook and cast out, and she keeps me company as we wait to see what we catch. It's so cool to think that someday these early lessons might be her first memories too.

# *Epilogue*

When we were faced with the reality of our crumbling marriage, we were very hard on ourselves and each other. We felt like failures, and we were profoundly scared of what the future held. We were both hurt and emotional; years of conflict and miscommunication and plain incompatibility had left us tired and raw. On our last days and through our last fights, we weren't saints. When we weren't lashing out at each other, we'd shut down completely. We were not best friends, and we were not beacons of understanding and emotional maturity. We were people in pain, gripped by fear, and we took it out on each other.

Divorce in general is a tinderbox of the two most explosive elements in human relationships, romance and finance, and ours was no different. Relationships shift and change all the time; love can morph from lust to romance to bitterness to platonic affection, often without skipping a beat. Everything was lined up to ensure we were going to be locked in a brutal battle for years. Our financial situation was convoluted and involved, even more difficult and personal than the average due to family business ties. Our son Asher was only three, and we both loved him dearly and had devoted our lives to him—a clear setup for horrible custody battles. We worried that it would be the worst divorce ever, the catastrophic event that would define our lives and, more critically, would define our son's life.

Even though we were as hurt, bitter, and scared as two humans can be, Asher's happiness and well-being meant everything to us. We just couldn't hurt him—so we didn't. We flat-out refused to take our parts in the stereotypical divorce narrative. We sat down together and dedicated ourselves to one guiding principle: We were going to do what was best for Asher. We committed to building something new, because we knew that no divorce we had ever seen would be good enough for our son.

There is no magic handshake, spell, or potion behind our family's success. It took a lot of hard work, smart thinking, and ego-swallowing. Not one of us is perfect, and getting to this point in our relationship was the hardest thing we've ever done. With more than a decade in the rearview mirror, we can say for certain that every ounce of effort we've put into making our divorce happy has not only been worth it, but necessary. We know it's been hard on Asher. He's definitely let us know over the years that packing up his life every few days, moving from house to house, and being away from one of us at any given time is tough. We have a happy divorce, sure, but it's still a divorce—and divorce sucks, particularly for kids. Acrimonious divorces magnify the types of hardships children deal with even more, and add on additional struggles when the children are stuck in the middle of two angry adults.

To give our child the love, stability, and hope we dreamed of, we needed to build a post-marriage life together that was better than our marriage had ever been. We weren't professionals, and we had no roadmap and no mentors. Although we have an amazing support network of friends and family, when we first announced our happy divorce intentions, no one quite got it. Many people wished us the best on this journey, and some offered every resource at their disposal, but until we got rolling, it all sounded like a desperate fantasy. Luckily, the two traits we share 100% are our deep, intense love for Asher and our stubbornness to the point of insanity.

It's a funny thing about compliments. Nothing can hold a candle to hearing from Asher how proud, excited, safe, loved, and inspired our new family dynamics have impacted him. He is in high school now, and when he handed us his application essay, we knew we had to share it. Here it is—uncoached and unedited.

*My parents have had such an amazing impact on my life. When I was young, my parents got divorced, and that may sound like a bad thing. In my case, it actually was not bad at all. My parents stayed best friends, and I ended up getting a stepmom, a stepdad, and a younger brother and sister. I have such a great relationship with all four of my parents, and now my mom and dad live on the same street. It is not ideal to have your parents divorced, but my family dealt with it very well, and I even got more influential people in my life.*

*My mom has had a very significant impact on my life since the day I was born. She is one of the reasons why I am who I am today. She has donated so much to many people in need and is a part of many different foundations and fundraisers, this has showed me to give generously and be very unselfish. My mom has also taught me to be kind to everyone by not just giving things, but by your actions. She has taught me to love others unconditionally. She truly has a heart of gold.*

*My dad has also been one of the greatest influences in my life. My dad and I have one of the greatest bonds I will ever have. He always tells me to work hard and never give up. He has taught me to do things with all of my ability and dedication. I owe my love of sports to him. They are a huge part of my life still today. One of the greatest things he has taught me is to never leave something once I have made a commitment to it.*

*My stepdad, Chad Chronister has had a huge impact on my life, just like both of my parents. Chad started off as a patrol deputy on the streets for The Hillsborough County Sheriff's Office almost 26 years ago. From hard work and dedication after working in so many different divisions from warrants, to narcotics, and even the SWAT team he has now been appointed to Sheriff. In his new role, he oversees about 4000 employees. This has taught me to aim high and to never doubt myself because hard work pays off. Chad has showed me how to protect, help and serve others and the community. All people are equal in his eyes.*

*My stepmom, Nadia Heldfond has also added great things to my life. She has had two kids, a daughter (Izzy) and a son (Jackson), since she and my dad married each other. She has always taught me to be a good older brother and to be a great role model for my siblings. Nadia has taught me to always help and do favors for others. Nadia is a great mom, and her parenting has showed me how I should act toward little children. Ever since I was four, Nadia has had a big impact on my life.*

*I am so fortunate to have such great and caring parents. They have always been good to me and they want what is best for me. They have also taught and showed me many helpful things. I not only have great parents, but also great stepparents. They are the reason for so many things in my life. I am who I am today because of all of my parents, and their influence on me.*

Twenty years have gone by since we met. It has been over a decade since we sat across from each other at that coffee shop, scared but stubborn, and decided to create the divorce and family we needed from scratch. The son we dedicated our lives to isn't a toddler anymore, and while some of our priorities have shifted, it's amazing how many have stayed the same. We want him to know he's loved, that we're always here if he needs to talk, that we're proud of him.

Everything we have and everything we do stems from our unconditional love for our children, and we want them to grow up surrounded by all the love and support they could ever need. Falling in love with people who loved Asher as much as we did and could commit to our plans seemed unlikely, but Chad and Nadia changed our minds. Our second marriages have only made our family stronger. We are all very different people, but we share a fierce conviction in our family and deep wells of love and honesty that make it work.

Inviting other people to join our family was a calculated risk; we had no room for pettiness, maliciousness, insecurity, or animosity. We're normal people—feelings get hurt, people get upset, and we drive each other crazy sometimes, but there are never any blow-up fights or passive aggressive nonsense. We never forget what it's all about and we regroup quickly.

It still hasn't always been smooth and easy—there have been some scary points when it seemed entirely possible that our family could fall apart unless we all worked together and found solutions. We had to consciously commit to our blended family during the worst moments, when the future looked uncertain and the effort to get there daunting. We all stepped up and took responsibility for the issues and for solving them. We were shocked by what we were capable of in action and how effectively we could solve problems as a team. Facing these challenges brought our family together and made it work on whole new levels, and we came out on the other side much happier and more confident in ourselves and each other.

Our blended family has grown and changed drastically over the years. We now share not one, but all three children, and we know we owe Izzy and Jackson the type of love, attention, and care we gave Asher. If our children look back on our modern family someday for inspiration, we hope they remember how valuable, rare, and rewarding a true sense of purpose is. We found ours in building this unique family, and we can confidently say that nothing in the world compares to realizing what you want most and fighting for it. We will always want what's best for Asher, Izzy, and Jackson. Our greatest hope for their futures is that they forge their own purposes and strike their own balances.

We use fairy tales to teach our children how incredible it is to do everything they think they can (and then the things they think they cannot), even when there are seemingly endless obstacles in their way, to find the people they love and the treasures no one else believed existed. We neatly tie up those fairy tales with happily ever after, but most people don't seem to put much stock in the happily ever afters in their own lives. We do; we know our divorce ended happily ever after, as did both of our second weddings, and every story in our lives since. Happily ever after doesn't mean the work is done: It is just the place where one story ends so another one can begin. Our lives are made up of many adventures, with many conclusions and many new beginnings. We're so thankful and proud that we have each other and our incredible blended family to welcome every happily ever after still to come.

If you are reading this book and going through a tough time, we trust that our story will give you hope that there is an easier, softer way.

As we said at the beginning of this book: Trust us. If we could do it, you can do it.

*Nikki DeBartolo*
*& Ben Heldfond*

# Acknowledgments

T here is no Happy Divorce without three people who play the most important role in this journey. First, our son Asher, to whom this book is dedicated. He was and is the motivation for us to put our big boy pants on, put our egos away, and dedicate ourselves to ensuring we do everything possible to not place the burden of divorce on his shoulders. Also, to our spouses, Nadia and Chad. You have both supported everything we have tried to accomplish without ever questioning it. We love you both very much and are so grateful for your acceptance and role in *Our Happy Divorce*.

To our parents, thank you for the lessons you have taught us. Without the foundation of love, honesty, respect and dedication you have passed on to your children, this divorce probably would not have had this outcome. From the day we told you we were getting a divorce, through the duration of the process, and to the current day, you have given us love, support and encouragement to not only your child in the relationship but also the in-law. Your commitment to what we were trying to accomplish is a major factor in our success.

To our friends (too many to mention), thank you for not judging or blaming either of us and instead supporting and loving us like we were still married.

In early 2016, we decided to write this book. Little did we know the process would take over three years and many revisions. We thought, *we will just write a book, no big deal.* Well, it is a big deal, and a lot harder than we thought. Not only the formation of complete sentences but the arrangement of the words posed many challenges. We could not have written this book without the help of our "book doctors," Maureen Lasher, Eric Lasher, and Lauren Kanne. Your patience and dedication to this project were second to none and we are forever grateful. Finally, thank you to Mascot Books for your patience and dedication to this project.